G000115752

BETTER

Advance Praise

"I've known Jeff for quite some time now, but reading this book allowed me to learn so much more about his personal story and allowed me to learn so much more about myself. It is eye-opening, uplifting, and inspiring. This is a must-read."

—WALT GEER III, EXECUTIVE CREATIVE DIRECTOR AT VMLY&R

"Jeff has a special way of helping people see the best in themselves. Better is the perfect book for anyone looking to stop hiding behind fear and walk into their future."

—KARLI BAROKAS, CEO AT BAROKAS COMMUNICATIONS

"I've known Jeff for close to twenty years. Jeff has this passion for helping people but, more importantly, he sees the best in people. Better is THE book for anyone looking to unlock a more purposeful, fulfilling future."

—BOB LANHAM, HEAD OF AUTOMOTIVE RETAIL AT FACEBOOK

"Jeff went beyond inspiring me, to teaching me why so many of us feel trapped in the first place—trapped by the so-called American dream, and by other people's expectations. With a big dose of reality, Jeff gives us permission to let go and become the best version of ourselves."

—LINDSEY WALENGA, CO-FOUNDER AND CEO OF SIREN STRATEGY

"Staring over the steering wheel knowing that there is
a better dream out there? Wonder how to take that first step?
And then the second? Better *provides insight, inspiration,
and the tough love necessary to get to . . . BETTER."*

—JIM FISH, ASSOCIATE PROFESSOR AT MIKE ILITCH SCHOOL OF BUSINESS
AND FORMER CHIEF INNOVATION OFFICER AT BOSCH

*"Jeff's passion for people stood out the
first day I met him and literally jumps off the page in* Better.
*If you're looking to unleash your superpowers and make a
difference in your world,* Better *is a great start."*

—JEFF BENNETT, CEO AT HIGI

*"Jeff has an uncanny ability to bring out a better side of people,
whether in person, through music, or through* Better.
The framework in Better *is a game-changer!"*

—ADELA PIPER, CO-FOUNDER AND CMO AT SIREN STRATEGY

*"If you've lost track of your dreams for a better life,
Jeff is here to help.* Better *will help you find a path forward for
a more fulfilling life at work and at home."*

—NED STAEBLER, CEO AT TECHTOWN DETROIT

BETTER

3 Steps to Shed Your Masks,
Own Your Freedom,
and Make "One Day" Today

JEFF PONDERS II

better.
M E D I A

Copyright © 2022 Jeff Ponders II
All rights reserved.

BETTER
3 Steps to Shed Your Masks, Own Your Freedom, and Make "One Day" Today

ISBN   978-1-5445-2767-3 *Hardcover*
           978-1-5445-2765-9 *Paperback*
           978-1-5445-2766-6 *Ebook*

To Charlie, JP3, Avery, and Xavier.

Together, we are better.

CONTENTS

FOREWORD

By Josh Linkner

Clutching his alto saxophone tightly, the intensity began to surge. Leaning back, knees bent, and swaying with the intricate rhythms of the drum set behind him, Jeff Ponders started to wail. Feverishly trying to keep up on the guitar, I glanced up at the captivated audience and noticed all eyes transfixed on the story being told from Jeff's horn. His improvised melodies conveyed the full range of emotion, from calm to fury, from determination to compassion. At the crescendo of his solo, he bounced up and down, expressing the joy of a child.

I'm not sure which was more noteworthy: the finale of his perfectly-timed creative expression or the exuberance of the crowd. On their feet and cheering with verve, this difficult-to-impress audience at the historic Cliff Bell's jazz club in downtown Detroit was roaring with delight.

With grace and humility, Jeff nods appreciation to the audience and then passes the musical baton to the piano player for his turn in the limelight. Jeff steps back with a nearly undetectable smile peeking through the right side of his mouth. The kind of knowing, confident look that a true master expresses when he knows he's delivered on his calling.

Jeff Ponders doesn't only reach such heights when playing jazz. In fact, he's achieved remarkable success in numerous areas of his life: from his time as an elite college athlete at the University of Pennsylvania to his entrepreneurial success as a digital pioneer scaling tech startups to his proudest accomplishment of all, his beloved family. Other people have achieved strong results, but Jeff has been able to do so while being grounded, peaceful, purposeful, and happy.

In the follow pages, Jeff shares the lessons he learned and the struggles he overcame to become such an exceptional musician, business leader, scholar, athlete, husband, father, and friend. He takes us on a journey, decoding success and liberating us from the traps that hold us back. He shows us how to be better—in both business and life—helping us lock our sights on our true calling and then pursue it with vigor.

I've had the pleasure of performing on dozens of stages with Jeff over the last twenty years. I've also seen him shine in business, in his community, and with his family. In *Better*, this modern-day renaissance man delivers a prescriptive approach for us all to elevate our performance in the pursuits we care about the most. Rich with detail, humor, and humility, the book delivers on the promise of helping us upgrade ourselves and those around us.

Better stands out from the endless sea of self-improvement and leadership books by revealing unexpected truths rather than spouting cliches and platitudes. It gives us the roadmap with grace, humility and compassion, just like author himself.

I was exhausted as we ended that set in the crowded Detroit jazz club, but Jeff's enthusiasm never waned. He was energized by creating, sharing, and contributing. His carefully placed notes and has masterfully developed ideas flowed as if his instrument was plugged directly into his soul, and the long line of fans waiting to shake his hand removed any question that Jeff was not only the master of his craft but was truly living his purpose. In this book, he's traded eighth notes for prose, arpeggios for words. Yet the same creative brilliance shines through each sentence, paragraph, and chapter.

It's been a delight to watch Jeff become *Better* over the last two decades, and I'm grateful that he's now generously sharing his wisdom to uplift us all. Take your time to careful read and absorb Jeff's insight, and you too will become *Better*.

—Josh Linkner, June 2021, Detroit, Michigan

ACKNOWLEDGMENTS

I'm grateful for a wonderful tribe that has supported me along my path to becoming better. First, to my heavenly Father: I'm humbled at my life's mission and each day I strive to walk in purpose. Thank You for the clarity of self, purpose, and passion.

To my family, Charlie, JP3, Avery, and Xavier: thank you for enduring countless days and nights of my maniacal creative sprints and obsessions with self-improvement. Yes, I'm sure I got on your nerves, but you accepted my journey as part of our journey. To my parents, Jeff Sr. and Debbra: thank you for modeling life transparently and candidly. You nurtured me to see people for both who they are and who they can become, and gave me the foundation to support and love them from point A to B. To my grandparents: it's part of my life's mission to uphold your legacy. To my parents-in-love, thank you for entrusting me with your legacy.

To Skyler, Jevon, Jericho, and the Scribe team: thank you for your incredible support! You pushed me to achieve more and I'm grateful. To Josh Linkner: you have often given me a glimpse into worlds that I didn't know existed while helping me see that it's reasonable to be Batman from time to time. To Mr. Mac: thank you for so many life lessons, few greater than remembering to keep faith first and to reject the ragtag. To Donald Walden and Marcus Belgrave: my life is infinitely better from your tutelage. I hope to uphold and honor your memory.

To Erro: thank you for the reminder to always trust the process. To Pastors Harvey Carey and Stan Rayford: thank you for seeing my heart and encouraging my work in the vineyard. To HotSauce: thank you for some of my greatest triumphs and most cherished memories. To Tyler, Art, Jocelyn, Otis, Darnell, Dave, and David: thank you for being the truest friends. Brandon, Dorsey, Allen, Berg, Rich, et al.: I'm grateful that a boy born an only child can grow up to be a man rich with brotherhood. To Alpha, Psi Chapter, GL, and the Rays: thank you for welcoming me into the school for the better making of men. To TechTown, IDV, Commune, Steamster, Siren, Live@, and every organization to whom I've been privileged to work alongside: thank you for accepting my gifts and my passions.

To the many entrepreneurs I've been blessed to support: thank you for sharing your dreams with me as you pushed to change the world. Your generosity allows me to operate in one of my highest callings. To my musical family: thank you for breathing melody to life. It's an honor to provide a soundtrack for the world with you. To my family and friends who are too many to name without sounding like a few chapters of the Bible: thank you. Your support and encouragement are a refreshing well of inspiration. To Detroit: thank you for supporting one of your many sons in my efforts to bring more light to the world from the Motor City.

To every person whom I've known, sat in a meeting with, or shared a conversation or a high five after a concert with: thank you for being in exactly the right place at the right time.

And to you, my reader, who is also at exactly the right place at this very moment: thank you for your attention and consideration. I pray these words were received with the love and intention with which they were crafted. My hope is that these principles leave an impression that empowers you to grow. I'm excited to hear how your world becomes better as you become better.

Peace and Love.

INTRODUCTION

I was twenty-three, with a business degree from Wharton, a great marketing job, and in the best health of my life. As I drove to work, watching a new sun kiss the Canadian skyline across the glittering Detroit river, miserable tears rolled down my face. I was living the American dream; it was a nightmare. I wanted out. All I wanted was out.

If your future feels like it's shrinking, if you're psyching yourself up to scratch and claw through each day knowing you're going to hate big chunks of it, if you've jokingly (or not) asked someone to "kill me now," I've been there. Breaking down under the weight of ongoing tragedy is understandable. Struggling against systemic injustice is noble. But finally having it all and hating it? Man, what's wrong with you?

Not one single thing.

It isn't you. Just like it wasn't me on that morning when I was crying in my car. How you feel isn't your fault, and it's not who you are. You didn't start out dreading each day, and you know that's not how life was intended to be. If you've worked hard and had some solid success, but you're starting to think the mountain you've been climbing all your life is made of paper—and it's starting to rain!—I've got you. And you're right—it doesn't have to be this way. There's more. Life can be BETTER. *You* can be BETTER. By being BETTER, I mean that:

You can be committed.

You can be healthy.

You can be present.

You can be intentional.

You can be accountable/responsible.

You can be heroic.

You can be better.

That's likely seven times better than you are today! Pretty cool, right?

So if you can't remember what you want but know this isn't it, or if you've given up on being who you wanted to be to get where you wanted to go, I've got a story and a simple, three-step process for you.

I started playing music when I was nine and was making money from it four years later. By the time I graduated from high school, I'd been recognized as one of the state's top saxophonists. I'd beaten out professional adults in competitions and was bringing in four figures a month playing gigs. I was having a blast, but I didn't know a musician around who was making the kind of bank I wanted to. Even in my teens, I had plans to be a multimillionaire. I'd had a full-ride scholarship to the University of Michigan waiting on me since my freshman year. I applied there and to Wharton and got into both. Michigan's business school was ranked fourth; Wharton's was first. I was ambitious. I went to Wharton.

It was an important decision, and I'll tell you more about it in Chapter 2, but the point here is that things started out well for me. My family wasn't wealthy, but by twenty-one (with some hefty student loans), I had a business degree and a band about to close a major record deal. A year after that, I was traveling the country playing music with my best friends, and I was killing it in sales for a Fortune 100 telecom. Three years later, I was bawling in my car. Then things got worse.

THE PROCESS

Whether you're just starting to see the cracks or falling apart, I'll use the story of my escape to a better life to help you put your life back together the way I did—stronger in the broken places. **BETTER**. The path from here to there consists of precisely three steps:

1. Seeing who you are

2. Envisioning who you could be

3. Becoming better

There's also a fourth bonus step that you'll continue taking for the rest of your life, but we'll get into that later.

I'm no longer living the dream—I'm dreaming up a better life every day. I'm living in the potential I felt as a kid and being my whole self in every aspect of my life. I'm free. I want the same for you. That's why I'm writing this book.

> Going to pieces looks different for everyone, but if you're feeling desperate or thinking about hurting yourself, please get immediate help. The National Suicide Prevention Lifeline can and does help. Call 800-273-8255 or use the chat feature at suicidepreventionlifeline.org. Please. You can always come back. I'm not going anywhere.

I'm not going to make you feel bad about yourself, but I'm not going to give you any excuses to stay as you are, either. *BETTER* isn't a miracle pill; it's a road to a better you. You've got to walk it yourself by implementing the process—but know I'm here, cheering you on. We're going to get there together.

Part life philosophy, part practical guide, *BETTER* is a guidebook for anyone ready to break the fuzzy handcuffs of "good job" bondage and shed the weight of the bland mask that's crushing your best features into corporate conformity. Whether you put on your mask for protection or conformity, to fit in at work, or get along with family, the principles I'll share can help you become your best and truest self in any relationship anywhere. I'm writing from the perspective of being authentic at work, but trust me—a mask is a mask and there's a reason they're scary. Stick with me, and let's watch the process work.

GETTING BETTER

We'll start by taking an open-eyed look at the American dream to see where it comes from and who benefits from it. Then I'll ask you to start thinking about your own dreams. I'll suggest a new definition of imposter syndrome, explore the mask and the superhero, and ask about your mask and your stories. We'll then discuss the setup for the breakdown and catalog some of corporate America's institutional insanities. You'll get a chance to shine a light on your own shadow, and I'll tell you why it isn't your fault if your life isn't the way you want it to be.

Next, we'll start on that three-step process I mentioned. I'll talk you through each step, ask you lots of questions, and give you some exercises designed to get you moving in the right direction. I'll suggest several different starting points depending on where you are and what feels most urgent to you. By the end of this book, you'll understand how to keep the becoming going and your ideal self growing to lock in your gains and to ensure your life continues to keep getting better and better as time goes on.

BETTER, for me, started with bad—crying, feeling like I'm dying in my car—and it only got worse from there. That's where our story starts.

Chapter 1

SELLING THE DREAM

I still don't know how it happened. After graduating from Wharton, I moved back to Detroit to start a company with my mom. From a long line of education-focused people and with a graduate degree of her own, Mom had been an entrepreneur for most of her professional life. With her experience and my business degree, we figured that working together was a great idea. Reality was less awesome. Charity may begin at home; maybe businesses shouldn't.

We both knew our scenario wasn't working, but you can't just quit on your mom. You can, however, accept a dream job when it lands in your lap on an otherwise average Wednesday in August. To be honest, I still don't know how they found me, but the timing was ideal—my student loans were coming due, and living at home was getting…let's go with "cramped."

I'd heard of the company—they were a global player in the ad industry, but I hadn't applied for the job, and my resume wasn't circulating out there. Still, when I read the job description, it felt like it was written with me in mind. I interviewed on Thursday; they made an offer on Friday, and I started on Monday.

It was my first big marketing job, and I was pumped! In the two years since I'd graduated, I'd done a lot. I'd chased my rock-star dreams across the country with my eight-piece band, won competitions, and built some serious momentum. I was looking forward to what promised to be an amazing career. Still, I hadn't let my formal education go to waste either. As much as I've always loved music, I love business too. I took a sales job with a Fortune 100 telecom straight out of school because I knew being good at sales was a prerequisite for business success. I was there for a year before I took the leap into entrepreneurship with Mom.

Our core idea was solid—a consulting practice focused on small business development in which we helped people launch and operationalize new companies. We did everything from business formation to bookkeeping and tax services to sales and marketing strategies. Mom had run a career consulting firm for years, helping people with backgrounds "from Yale to jail, Park Avenue to park benches." She coached her clients on everything from crafting resumes to negotiating salaries. She has a real genius for helping people land opportunities they can see but don't feel qualified to reach for. I've always had a passion for helping early-stage business owners figure out how to grow, and I'd done similar consulting work while I was in college. It was a service people needed. We were highly qualified and philosophically committed to offering it. We lasted two days.

Okay, it might have been more like a couple of months, but our new-business high was very short-lived. Take it from me, at twenty-three, living and working with your mom is not the path to family harmony. When that Wednesday morning call came with its ideal-for-me job title, a generous salary, and a Get Out of (mom)-Jail Free card, I jumped in with both feet. It was my dream job, after all, my very own version of the American dream. What else was I going to do?

When I talk about that kind of dream—the dream job, the American dream—you know what I mean, don't you? But where does it come from? Whose dream is it, and who benefits from the power that dream has over our national imagination? More importantly, how does that dream turn into a nightmare, how does its promised freedom come to enslave us, and what can we do about it?

The American dream was never the bright vision of a better life for everyone who arrived on our country's shores "yearning to breathe free." You don't have to look any further than the cargo of slave ships to see that. The American dream is a modern invention, built on a universal human substrate, one that's outlived any nobility it may have had when it was first imagined. And, make no mistake, that American dream is dreaming us, not vice versa. If we're looking for BETTER, we'll need to build a better dream.

As with any renovation project, our first step in building a better dream is deconstructing the old structures.

THE AMERICAN DREAM

You know the formula: do well in school so you can get into a good college so you can find a good job and have a good life. We all grow up with this message, this understanding. Even if our parents didn't bottle-feed it to us, it hangs suspended in the oxygen Americans breathe. Wealth equals success. A good job equals a good life. What you do is who you are. And maybe this is true for some people. Certainly, for many people, like my dad, education has been a path out of poverty and into a more secure life for his children.

I'm here to tell you the dream is a lie.

The American dream benefits the folks who created and sell it, not those who work and strive for it every day. It isn't meant for us. It was developed generations before we were born by men living a reality that we'll never experience. I lived that dream myself for more than half of my life before I noticed it was there. Before I realized it was dreaming me.

The Employment Dream

The American dream isn't uniquely American, but it isn't universal either. It's only about two hundred years old—just about exactly as old as this country. Before the Industrial Revolution, for hundreds (if not thousands) of years, the workforce looked radically different than it does today.

The vast majority of people who've ever lived on this planet worked small family farms or practiced a trade. They took their goods to market or lived above shops where people came to them for the candles or barrels or horseshoes they made. Community was built into commerce, and families directly handed down professions with the necessary education and implements—from parent to child or master to apprentice. With few exceptions, everyone worked in a small business that served the community where they lived. Stability came from land ownership or craftsmanship, and the purpose of money was to buy what you couldn't make yourself.

Everything changed with the Industrial Revolution. With the introduction of new materials like iron and steel and new energy sources like coal, steam, and electricity, factories replaced farming, and mass manufacturing replaced the handicraft economy. As businesses got larger, the idea of the employee was born, and more and more people left the land and shops they owned to move into rapidly growing cities where they worked for wages—wages which they now depended upon as their sole means of survival. People no longer built their own houses or grew even a portion of their own food. Houses were built and food was grown by workers employed by owners who sold the houses and food to workers who were paid by other owners for their work building cars or weaving cloth that the construction and farm workers paid to drive and wear. That's how it is now, but it's not how it's always been or how it has to be.

The Education Dream

With this titanic shift from the worker/owner to workers and owners, education changed from providing the basic math and literacy people needed to operate their own businesses to delivering the training that owners needed their workers to have. Initially, this training was in the unsubtle arts of obedience, timeliness, and dependability that factory owners needed. While many of those values linger, today the focus is on training those skills required by the corporate world.

Every year, nearly four million students matriculate from college, many as part of their pursuit of the American dream. They're hoping—genuinely, fervently hoping—to leverage their education (and years' worth of debt) to get a good job in which they make good money. The education dream isn't a pipe dream—it's relatively realistic, as far as dreams go—it's a pipeline dream, the American dream's predicate. Education today pipes students into the business world, having promised that a good education will yield a good job working for a good company earning good money to buy goods other companies pay other workers to make.

If you're reading this book, you're probably at least a few steps down this path. Maybe you've graduated from college or maybe you haven't, but I'll bet you have a job working for a company. You probably have an at-will agreement with your employer, so your job security isn't secure—it barely even exists. Odds are you don't have union protections either. You may be okay with what you're earning, you may even feel like you're getting away with something, but I'll bet you know that the people who own the company you work for are taking home an amount with more commas than you're getting. Is that unfair? Not really.

The Owner's Dream

The people who own companies, in effect, own and operate systems for creating value. Ray Kroc had a decent hamburger and fries (which are still amazing), and his company, McDonald's, could have done what hundreds of other small restaurants had already done, but he found a way to do it at scale. Ray Kroc had a vision of delivering a consistent burger-and-fries experience to people across the country and, eventually, the world. He had a dream, and he built a system to make that dream a reality. He deserved to be compensated for that.

It isn't necessarily wrong that Ray Kroc made millions on that system while hiring others to operate it for a tiny fraction of what he made. People with unique dreams who execute on their vision and found new companies or build new systems create value and should be rewarded for doing so. When those people identify roles that need to be performed to create and maintain their companies, it only makes sense for them to fill those positions as cheaply as possible relative to the complexity of the work. When people who have made their dreams into companies create such roles, they're called jobs. By definition, having a job means you're filling a role that helps to make someone else's dream real.

THE HALF-TRUE DREAM

Whereas most people worked for themselves once upon a time, today most of us work for business owners, having been carried to their offices by the education pipeline, which we entered chasing the American dream. When we arrived, we took jobs we worked to make the dream of the owners come true.

Am I saying we're all stupid? No way! What makes this dream so night-marish is that it's partially true. The promise that brought people into cities for factory jobs is the same promise that sent me to Wharton. It's a promise that was never extended to the thousands of generations that were born before steel and mass production—the promise of upward mobility.

It's the promise that drives the dream—if you're committed and if you work hard and if you're willing to do what it takes—you really can get what you want. The hardest-working farmer five hundred years ago couldn't hope for much more than to get through the winter a little less starved than his neighbor. Today, he can go from obscurity to celebrity in the time it takes to compose a Tweet or snap a picture.

The nightmare twist to the American dream is this: they've convinced us that "whatever we want" is what they want us to want.

The Consumer Dream

In our post-Industrial world where corporations and their owners have co-opted the American dream for themselves and sold us on an education-to-job pipeline that delivers us to work for them, the dream of a better life becomes the dream of better stuff. Children are swaddled in advertising and weaned on purchases. Their most primal infant needs are satisfied by things their parents buy in stores. They play with toys that are appropriately scaled models of the cars and houses they're being trained to dream of buying.

Maybe explicitly, maybe vaguely, they hope to eventually meet a *good* match they can marry before buying a *good* house in which to raise their *good* kids. Upon those children's births, they'll start saving to send them to a *good* college. They'll also keep saving for their *good* retirement so they can move to Florida and play golf and sip beer in the *good* weather, looking back on how *good* life was to them. They'll make their assessment of the *good*ness of their life based on how closely it hewed to the good consumer's dream. Good enough, right?

Our earliest dreams are shaped to fit the consumer dream that keeps the owners' dreams alive, but we can't stop dreaming. Dreams are necessary. The natural order for all living organisms is growth, and dreams tell us the direction in which we want to grow. Kids want to be grown-ups. The longing for growth is innate, and a sense of progress is inextricably bound up with happiness. And that's where it gets tricky.

The Good-Enough Dream

Eventually, we stop growing in the literal sense (or we'd never fit into our shoes), but if we don't keep metaphorically growing, if we don't keep making progress, it's simply impossible for us to be happy. I'm not sure what it is about our culture that makes this more apparent in the physical domain. We all recognize what happens to our bodies as we age if we don't exercise—nothing good! So we go to the gym where we make ourselves uncomfortable. We stress our bodies. We push ourselves. Weightlifting tears muscle tissue to force it to grow. We increase our reps or run longer distances to keep making progress. Or we don't. We trade struggle and growth for comfort. "Great" takes work. "Good enough" is easy. Good enough is poison.

Don't drink the good-enough poison!

The hand-me-down dream is good enough. We settle for it because it's readily available and requires just enough effort to feel earned and because a reluctance to hold out for something better has been drip-fed to us right along with the American dream. Often by the people who love us the most. Parents see a kid who's upset because he got a B on a test when he wanted an A or the one who's crying because she came in second in the forty-yard dash. Parents hate to see their children hurting, and they point out (rightly) that 3.0s and silver medals are still good, but there's a big difference between good and good enough and between "you can try to beat your own record next time" and "be happy with what you did." There's no conflict between good and better, but *good enough* is how the hands of *great* get tied.

CORPORATE BONDAGE

As the Industrial Revolution shifted workers from the farm to the factory, the work of agriculture—growing plants for food and fabric—moved from the small family farm to the plantation, which drove demand for two things: huge landholdings and cheap labor. America was ideally suited to meet those demands. It rose to its position as a world economic power on the strength of its enormous size and the imported labor of slaves. Say what you like about our country's foundational ideologies of freedom and equality, but its wealth and economy are firmly rooted in slavery.

When slavery ended, the labor system that replaced it retained many aspects of the owner-worker dynamic. While corporations no longer feel entitled to beat or kill their workers, they still attempt to exert a great deal of control over our lives. In the same way there were once field slaves and house slaves, today there are blue- and white-collar laborers.

To owners, field slaves were low-level, interchangeable workers who were easily replaced, and in whose well-being they were, at best, disinterested. House slaves, on the other hand, who were more acculturated and more compliant, were seen as more highly skilled and more valuable, and they were treated better and lived longer. They didn't precisely have 401(k) plans or more vacation days (or any, for that matter), but they did get more privileges and were, consequently, more loyal. If they didn't believe in the system, they would at least defend their positions within it and occasionally side with their owners when the field workers tried to escape or revolt. The house slaves were what the field slaves hoped their children could be, while they dreamed (as all parents do) of their freedom.

There are many ways in which the modern corporation is the new slave field. (Spoiler alert: we'll come back to ideas of servitude and freedom several times throughout these pages.) But for me—and I imagine for most of you reading this—the shackles of our employment are closer to novelty-store furry handcuffs than to the chains of true slavery.

Your job is your kink.

Furry handcuffs look like fun. You hold out your wrists and willingly have them put on, thinking you're in for a good time. Then one day, get a peek out from under the blindfold, and you have no idea where you are or how it all got so boring. And your hands are still tied.

The Freedom Dream

I'd gone to college with the idea of buying my freedom. Instead, I sold it because the "dream job" looked like fun. Besides, handcuffs come with "at-will employment" keys. I was crying on my commute to a job I could leave at will because I'd given up my power to do anything different. It wasn't the job that held me captive; it was the entire apparatus of the American dream. It was the student loans for my good education, the salary for the good life, and the payments on the good car I was crying inside of.

Maybe the worst thing about the plush handcuffs of the American dream is that the group dream smothers the individual one. With the human need for growth yoked by the dream's ability to motivate and guide, and spurred on by our natural preference for comfort, we settle for the good-enough American dream that kinda sorta fits because it's comfortable (or furry) enough. But dreams aren't, and can't be, one-size-fits-all.

THE INDIVIDUAL DREAM

Real, non-metaphorical dreams are deeply personal. They're conjured while you sleep by some mysterious, deep part of yourself and unspool before you in the private theater of your mind. The programming of your subconscious streaming service can be influenced by the larger stage of the real world. Still, once a dream starts, it is its own world, and you're its only inhabitant, as well as its actor, director, and writer.

Of course, your parents have hopes for and visions of your future. Your managers and mentors have probably laid out paths for you to follow based on what they think you want. But real dreams are utterly individual. Even when you write them down immediately upon waking or relate them to the one person who knows you best, they're hard to communicate. There's no dream broadcasting app yet (although I'm sure eventually someone—or some AI—will code some creepy, *Black Mirror* version of one), and until then, no one can truly share their dreams. Your real dreams are exclusively and intimately personal. Your life dream can and should be too.

I cordially invite you to screw the American dream. It wasn't meant for you. It was developed generations before you were born by men living a reality you'll never experience. It benefits only the folks who created and sell it, not those who work and live it every day. The rich sell the freedom dream to support their freedom and encourage the work of others. You don't have to buy in. You can dream your own dreams.

Your Dream

Don't panic! I'm not going to ask you to write down your individual dream right now. We'll get there. It's fine if you don't have any idea where to start at this moment. In fact, most people don't know what they truly want out of life. We've spent our lives having our individual dreams sucked out of us to make room for the insertion of an entire colony of employment, education, owners', half-true, consumer, good-enough, and freedom dreams. No wonder it's hard to hear our own voice in that crowd.

It's as if we're all bonsai trees, with our natural urge to dream snipped and shaped by our parents, educational system, and consumer culture. A bonsai is encouraged to grow, but only in specific directions and into certain shapes. Nobody asks the bonsai tree what it wants.

Dear Bonsai,

What does the good life mean to you?

SHOPPING FOR DREAMS

Now we've taken a good, hard look at the dream profiters who very effectively capitalized on the human need for dreams to direct our instincts toward growth. It's a post-Industrial dream created by owners and fed by the educational pipeline, which lures us inside as children weaned on the American dream.

As I drove to work that first Monday morning of my new marketing job, I believed I was living the dream. Several years later, in tears on that same drive on a different day, I woke up and realized my job had become a nightmare that was dreaming me. As I took a more open-eyed look at the American dream and came to see it for what it was, I began to imagine a better dream that might replace it—a dream built for me and by me. Now, I'm inviting you to do the same. You don't need to pick up your hammer (or even your pen) just yet. For now, it's enough to let your subconscious mind ponder what your dream of the good life might be.

The American dream is a fairy tale we've been sold where "And they lived happily ever after" has been replaced with "Got a good job." Life, however, keeps on going after you get that good job. Once you've accomplished that, what are you meant to do with the years left in the story of your life?

To find out, you need to go back to where all stories start.

Chapter 2

TELLING THE ORIGIN STORY

Every superhero from Spiderman to Jesus has an origin story—something extraordinary (spider bite or virgin birth) that happened early in life and set up their destiny. You have one too. It's probably not quite as dramatic; I know mine wasn't. Still, these stories have commonalities: they start at the beginning and reveal our individual plotlines and themes—which are all too easy to miss from the midstream of the narrative. You have to take a few steps back to see them. Once you do, you're able to take a more active role in telling the rest of the story.

Origin stories also include an event that shifts the protagonist into a hero. These transitions are always painful and usually require a dismantling of the hero, almost as complete as the one we just performed on the American dream.

Tracking our individual, personal stories from our childhood dreams through their mutation into plans that function as subplots within the larger American dream sets the stage for a transformation from which a hero can emerge.

In this chapter, I'll tell my story from my earliest interest to my full-blown love affair with music. It's a personal story, but I'm sharing it to illustrate how even a story that begins with its dreams fiercely protected by followers of the truest parts of the American dream can find its protagonist with a compound dream living a subplot plan. That's where I was when the radioactive spider (or shipwreck or super-soldier-building secret program) got me. I'll share that story and chronicle my transformation, not into a hero but a company man.

Because my story lives inside the larger American narrative, I believe it has more to offer than a simple illustrative parable. We'll back out from the personal to examine how the corporate world interacts with individual dreams and how it compensates for the letdown most people experience when "happily ever after" drags on, delivering on the *ever* if not the *happy*. We'll look at how owners hold onto workers and what that confinement does to us.

MY STORY

Music lives at the core of my earliest memories. It's integrated with my fundamental self so vitally and inextricably that it feels like a part of my soul. Music runs in my family but always seemed particularly concentrated in me. My parents sang in the church choir, and I had a grandmother and cousins who played instruments, but I'm the kid who remembers the music at Disney World more than the rides. I was obsessed with Michael Jackson (maybe not as much as some…no sparkly glove for me, thanks), but I knew all of his songs, including both the lyrics and the dance moves—even to "Thriller," a song that terrified me. I stuck with it anyway, because it was MJ, and dang, those zombies could dance!

When early aptitude tests flagged me as musically gifted, my parents started me in piano lessons. I liked piano well enough, but when I was nine, the saxophone found me. It reached right out of the radio during a Kenny G song and grabbed me by the throat. I remember thinking, not "I can do that" or "I want to do that," but "I *will* do that." I lobbied everyone, and eventually my aunt bought me my first sax. From the minute I picked it up, my relationship with music changed. It went from love to obsession. Music just fit me—or I fit it. Either way, we bonded for life.

I'm not sure how obvious my obsession with music was from the outside. It was hardly my only after-school activity. I played basketball and soccer and was already experimenting with entrepreneurship, but all the time, I was practicing music. And I do mean practicing! I don't think my parents had any idea how good I was getting because all they heard at home was the sound of me working through the toughest bits over and over. They probably thought I was struggling, but I was in love, and even the hard work felt like play.

When I started middle school, I tried out for the beginner band but was moved up to first chair saxophone in the top band by the end of the first week. By the time I graduated from high school, I was one of the top saxophonists in the state, making four figures doing something I loved. I wanted to keep playing music, but my dream wasn't just to be a musician. That's a simple (if not an easy) dream. It's never easy to be excellent at anything, but what I wanted was also more complex. I wanted two things—to build companies and play music. And even then, as a confident young man with a string of wins and no real losses, I knew that a compound dream was riskier than a singular one.

MY DREAM

I remember the calculus of my dream very clearly: Money = Freedom. I wanted the financial freedom to go all-in on building companies and making music. In high school, my AP Economics teacher had made it very clear that investing in the stock market was the only way billionaires who weren't born were made. Even on that path, though, you need money to make money, and I wasn't exactly in a position to play music and the markets and get rich that way. All the investors I saw were traders and investment bankers. I decided I needed to work on Wall Street to make the kind of money I figured it would take to buy the degree of freedom I wanted to have. So off I went to Wharton.

I could have gone to Michigan and studied music and business, but Wharton was the top business school in the country, and I wanted the best. I also knew that networking was different in the Ivy League schools—plus, I wanted to move out of state for a while. I recognized that a person can't give 100 percent to two things. There has to be some kind of split. Choosing Wharton was absolutely a choice that I was not choosing music right then. Sure, I kept practicing, took a couple of lessons, and played in a few groups on campus, but I was more focused on getting the full Wharton experience rather than on trying to satisfy both passions. Besides, I still had my band in Detroit and was able to scratch that itch to perform over every school break.

I wanted the best and recognized the sacrifice that takes.

The Wharton pipeline trades in vastly different numbers than the automotive one I'd seen growing up in Detroit, and initially, it looked pretty good to me. Wharton grads typically go to Wall Street, Silicon Valley, or top-tier consulting firms. At first, that was what I wanted: starting with a summer internship making $40,000 in four months and graduating at twenty-one into a job where I would make between $80,000 and $100,000 per year, not to mention a potential bonus of up to $200,000. But once I got an up-close look at that life—at the fourteen-hour days, six days a week, fifty weeks a year—I realized it was not what I wanted, after all.

I was willing to work hard to buy my freedom, but my plan had never been sequential. I didn't want to quit music for fifteen years to get rich and then go back to playing music. I was willing to prioritize, to set up the money, but not to abandon music in the present to get to play in the future. Besides, I was in my twenties and wanted to have some fun!

Since I wanted music *and* business, I started looking at the music business during my time at Wharton. I started bringing guest speakers onto campus and working with the Grammy Foundation. I did some work for a jazz PR firm and interned at a record label where DJ Jazzy Jeff was my boss. I started to piece it together, merging my passions for music and business. When I graduated, I decided to go back to Michigan. My band was on track to land a major record deal, and I planned to take a curation approach to building my career.

At Wharton, I'd done some paid consulting work with startups and discovered I most enjoyed working with new and small companies. Back in Detroit, I set out to build the skills, experience, and relationships I'd need to help me build effective companies. The plan was to build businesses and be in a band. I had a dream, and I curated my experiences to accelerate my ability to make that dream real. I took each job with two primary outcomes in mind: to learn what I needed to know to move my dream forward and provide value where I was.

That out-of-nowhere phone call seemed heaven-sent in part because the job I was being offered looked like the perfect next step in my plan. I excelled in sales with my first job, and next on my list was to develop my marketing chops. Landing a role in strategy at a leading digital marketing agency wasn't just a great job: it was the perfect next step. I worked my tail off and enjoyed every minute. I liked what I was doing, and I did it well. I was building the skills I needed; I got along well with my boss, team, and clients; and, before I knew it, I was up for my first promotion.

I didn't get it.

Even my boss was upset—we'd both been expecting that I would get the promotion. After all, as she pointed out, both my peers and my clients loved me, I was a leader on my team, and everyone agreed I was doing excellent work. The only negative comment on my performance review was that I spent my time outside of work playing music—which had nothing to do with my performance. It was simply my company's perception of my personal life that was standing in my way. Maddeningly, their perception wasn't even right. I wasn't out playing music every night at that point—half of my band was out touring with a Grammy-nominated artist. But in the minds of the powers that be, people who were serious about success in the corporate world didn't do anything else.

My dream was too big. I couldn't have it all. I was given a hundred-dollar gift card and told I could be a real rock star at work if I gave up being one in real life.

MY GOOD JOB, THE END

Once the pipeline delivers you from the educational system to the corporate world, it hits a snag. Part of what makes the American dream so compelling is that it plays into the human need for recognition and growth. Once you arrive, to a certain extent, those incentives evaporate. "Get a good job" is the ultimate goal of the sixteen-plus years of education with its orderly progression from grade to grade and the clear feedback letter grades provide. When you join the workforce, those markers and rewards are replaced with a much hazier set of possible promotions and performance reviews. "Get a good job" morphs into "Get a better job." The positive is replaced with the comparative, with no ultimate superlative in sight. There is no final "best" you can reach and be done with the race. It's a treadmill, not a track.

This is usually the point when the "Is this all there is?" feeling sets in. We work so hard to get that good job, believing a good job equals happiness —but it doesn't. Most people are happier working toward that good job than they are in the job once they get it. In part, this is because the job we're working predates us. You were hired because there was a hole that needed to be filled, and you were the best fit that could be found. Your job wasn't made to fit you, but don't worry, they'll reshape you to fit it.

Companies have two levers they can pull—two fundamental human needs they can manipulate to mold their raw recruits into good corporate soldiers. One is progress: the progressively better job with the incrementally increasing salary we've already discussed. The other is recognition.

The desire to be recognized and praised for our efforts is so fundamental that it's one of my most powerful parenting tools. I know it won't always be this effective. One day, my son's peers' good opinion may matter more to him than my praise or condemnation. But right now, he's five years old and wants me to be happy with him, so a "good job" from Daddy goes a long way.

Social validation and praise for a job done well are necessary (if not necessarily enough) for happiness. We want recognition for a job well done, and when we put in the work and aren't acknowledged, it feels like rejection. And social rejection hurts. It affects how we feel, how we think, and even our physical health. Our need to belong is a drive rooted in our evolution, as strong as those for food and water. Humans rely on social groups for survival, and our need for acceptance is no different from our hunger for food. It's a survival mechanism. We all want to fit in, but few of us are culture- or cubicle-shaped.

Companies want to help us slot neatly into the roles they have open. Having hired individual humans, companies are happy to help us become their human resources. They'll cheerfully teach us how to suit their culture and provide financial and social incentives to encourage us to do so. But is it really what we want? Certainly, no one wants to be an outcast, but fitting in and being cast out aren't the only options.

I believe that when you live your own dream, it takes you to places you can belong. Belonging is fundamentally different from fitting in. When you belong, the job fits itself to you. It's the difference between finding a company to work for and finding one that works for you.

*Fitting in is good enough. Belonging is **BETTER**.*

Getting turned down for that promotion shifted my focus. My driving question became "What do I need to do to be recognized?" It's not a terrible question; the hitch is that I knew the answer—I needed to be someone I wasn't. I wasn't willing to give up music (I'm not sure I could if I tried), but I'd gotten the message—*who* I was wasn't an asset at work.

That hurt. It felt exactly like the rejection it was—not of my performance or my results but of my identity. They made clear that who I was would cost me the price of recognition and progression through the ranks.

I'm a naturally ambitious person, but I don't believe in the zero-sum game theory. I don't need someone else to lose for me to win. I do need to regularly beat my previous performance. I want to see growth. I understood what they were asking of me, but I wanted that promotion—the new title, the increased salary, and the recognition. And I was willing to do what was necessary to get it. I didn't spot the irony at the time, but my desire to be recognized came at the cost of hiding who I was. I decided to shear my work self off from the rest of my life and put on the ill-fitting mask of the Company Man.

THE COMPANY MAN

The company man wears company T-shirts and goes to company events. He stays later than required—not necessarily to do extra work, but to be seen putting in the extra hours. I started logging in to Instant

Messenger at night from rehearsal halls or gigs. I participated in conversations on the authorized topics: spouse/kids, local sports teams, recent TV shows, or movies. I didn't talk about entrepreneurship. I didn't talk about music. I played with Kanye West one night, went into work the next morning, and didn't mention it.

The company man does not have outside passions. The company is his everything, and the company likes it that way. The company is a jealous lover and feels insecure if other things might satisfy those human needs it uses to hold onto you. Worse, a person who's happy in his life outside of work suggests to the other company men by his example that there might be more to life than the company can provide.

The company man conforms. He shaves off the bits of himself that don't fit into the company cubicle. He keeps his conversation topics and intensity anodyne. If the company finds his hair or way of speaking incongruent with the image it feels the need to project, the company man will comply when asked to change.

Most companies that are proudly cubicle-free have a vision of what they do and how they do it. Often, they call this vision "culture" or their "way of working." It's what defines them as a business, and it gets handed down from leadership. People applying for work are evaluated against it and hired if they are deemed a good fit. And that determination of whether a potential new hire fits is too often made on the most superficial evidence. In your fifties? You're not going to be considered for a company with a "youth culture."

Even companies claiming diversity as part of their culture frequently define the term by homogeneous criteria—gender and color—while failing to notice their entire workforce is physically attractive, politically liberal, monolingual, and young. These companies would never ask someone to cut their hair or temper their accent; they just don't bring them back for the second interview once they see or hear the applicant. The question is still: do you fit us? If it isn't one-size-fits-all of the broader American dream, it's still one-size-fits-us, and the company man makes that work.

Once hired to fit a cubicle or a culture, our roles are defined by the company based exclusively on what it needs, not on what else we might offer. I have a friend whose capabilities not only met but far exceeded what his work asked of him. He was doing everything his manager needed, and they both agreed he was doing it well. He enjoyed the work and was celebrated for it. When he spotted a new and exciting opportunity space where he thought the company might prosper, he went to his manager and asked her if, in addition to what he was already doing, he could start to position himself to execute on the new opportunity. She turned him down. The company didn't need him operating in any additional capacity, only the one for which they'd hired him. The company man brings to the company only what it needs. He hides the rest behind the mask.

YOUR MASK (OR YOUR SHOES)

For some reason, beginning in the Tang Dynasty, the female ideal in China started to include having very (very) small feet. Hoping to raise their status, and thereby their marriage prospects, mothers bound their daughters' feet so tightly and from such a young age that their toes literally grew backward into the soles of their feet. That's right, mothers lovingly and deliberately deformed their children in accordance with what society found valuable. We do the same thing to ourselves psychologically when we constrain who we are for the sake of our work, its paycheck, and status. Like feet that don't stop growing, we cripple ourselves to fit our work boots.

How many of those maimed Chinese girls would have been accomplished runners or dancers had they been allowed to develop feet that could support them? How many of us let our unique and beautiful gifts atrophy from lack of use, unable to find a place at work to flex them? Those competencies and interests, talents, and training make us unique and fulfilled but, if they are not of value to our employers, they get forced back into our souls.

Dear Foot Soldier,

What parts of you don't fit behind your company mask or are being deformed by someone else's ideals?

MAKING UP STORIES

Every life is a story with a beginning, middle, and end, but not every protagonist tells their own story or becomes their own hero. Understanding how your story started and tracking its separate narrative threads, themes, and supporting characters prepare you to have more of a voice in its telling. It can also help you begin to assemble the hero you want to be from the pieces left by whatever arachnid, accident, or admin blew you apart. In Chapter 4, we'll dig into your personal history to better understand who you are and where you come from. For now, start imagining your past as a story you've been told and are brushing up on as preparation to start writing your future yourself.

Chapter 3

WEARING THE MASK

We put on a mask whenever who we are isn't appropriate to where we are. And that's fine. We all have multiple social masks, and nobody is (or should be) the same person on the basketball court and in church. But if you're going to spend more of your awake hours at work than anywhere else (and you probably are), the mask you wear there needs to be pretty lightweight or not necessary at all.

That wasn't how it worked out for me. Because my actual face was the one I couldn't show, I started wearing my work face the way Peter Parker and Bruce Wayne wear masks—not to protect them (latex won't deflect a punch) or to give them special powers (those come from spiders, bats, and emotional trauma, respectively)—but to hide their true identities.

Superheroes wear masks to keep ordinary people from knowing who they are. I'm not sure why, but it seems incredibly important to keep the extraordinary separate from the ordinary. If you're a god from another realm or a foundling from a different planet, you can wear a human face *as* a mask, but if you're an ordinary person with extraordinary abilities, you have to hide your face behind a mask that breaks your life into segments.

The corporate nightmare mask fractures a life into convenient single servings that are sized for the office cubicle. A life too large or too resilient to stand that tidy division eventually breaks down and breaks free. It's an excruciating process, but when you can finally see your true face in the mirror, you can start the process of becoming your own hero.

In this chapter, I'll share the story of my mask's fracturing and explore the forces that contribute to a particular kind of postdream breakdown. I'll give you a list of warning signs and talk you through what happens when the mask's weight becomes unsustainable. I'll give you questions to ask yourself and introduce you to the tools you'll use to recover and begin creating something better.

FRACTURING

After my performance review, I started leaving big parts of myself at home when I went to work. I stuffed what didn't fit behind the mask, determined to make it work for me. After all, it was still a great job that allowed me to do work I enjoyed with clients I liked for good money. But if I could go back and talk to the young man I was then, I'd tell him, "It's not supposed to work for you. You're not made for it, and, more importantly, it's not made for you."

Putting energy and effort into a job that wasn't made for me meant that I was essentially working against myself. It felt like walking into a heavy headwind. I kept pressing forward while everything else in my life pulled at me, trying to drag me toward those things that spoke to my heart and soul.

I lived behind my corporate nightmare mask for a long time before I realized I no longer recognized myself. I was doing all the things I thought I wanted to do at one of the leading global marketing agencies. The mask was doing its job. I learned how to fit the system and landed a role with the coolest job title—VP of Innovation—and was set up to lead teams that helped drive business for dynamic companies. I'd recently led a team of executives from a Fortune 500 company through a plan to ready their organization for the future. They'd loved it. They said all the right things but never took action. Every project I had, I pushed for the kind of innovation I was supposed to be vice president of, and nothing ever changed. Work was hollow, and my mask was too tight.

While most people can sustain the stress of being someone they're not or keeping parts of themselves separate for a while, eventually it catches up to them. They don't recognize who they've become, and they get depressed or become resentful.

Putting on the mask is the setup for The Breakdown. The Breakdown is different for different people, but it all comes from the same place. It comes from trying to fracture your whole and beautiful self into bits small enough to fit it into cubicles or cultures and to mask your bare-faced truth from people who don't want to see your superpowers.

The corporate mask is a thing of nightmares. The longer we wear it, the tighter it clings to our true face as it decays. Mine did its outside job, but it did a job on me. I started to hate what was otherwise a great job because I didn't like the guy it made me pretend to be.

I had the corporate mask that I wore at work—one I'd chosen to put on—but I'd grown another like a shell over my skin without really noticing. It was the "I'm okay" mask. I quit looking at myself without it, even when I was alone in front of the bathroom mirror. I insisted on it, even as I swore it wasn't there. "No, that's just my face—my happy, okay face." But my wife saw it—cracked and peeling, with rage oozing out at all the seams.

I was angry, and I was empty.

I still loved music, and I never stopped playing gigs, but I wasn't having as much fun with them, and I'd stopped participating in some of the organizations I'd been a part of. Every day, I woke up feeling heavy and dragged on that corporate mask, thinking, *Here we go again.* And underneath that thought was a soft whisper: *Something's got to give. You can't keep doing this, again and again, every day for the rest of your life.*

The weight of that mask, the strain of trying to be Work Jeff and Everywhere Else Jeff began to tear me apart. It almost had to. How else could I be in both places? It felt like hell's version of the "rub your belly, pat your head" game. I was fragmenting and didn't realize it until I finally fell apart. As a person who took real pride in always having it together, being in pieces was a humbling experience.

I don't remember what finally cracked, only that it was a moment of acute, holistic frustration with my life and work that punctured the swelling bubble of internal, unacknowledged, existential terror. It broke me open, which looks a lot like breaking down.

The floor rose up and hit me, or my knees quit doing their job. I lay on the kitchen floor, curled into a ball, and I lost it.

BREAKING DOWN THE BREAKDOWN

A breakdown can look like drinking too much or going postal. It can show up in slowly degrading performance or increasing risk-taking. Expressions like "kill me now" and "FML" sound like jokes, but they can be the sounds of someone starting to splinter. People use mood-altering drugs, prescribed or otherwise. They self-medicate with food that drives obesity and spending that racks up debt. They eat things they have no appetite for, buy things they don't need, and sleep with people they shouldn't, and they get fatter, deeper in debt, and divorced.

They're rotting from the inside because their nightmare mask is screwed on too tight, and the person they actually are can't breathe.

I'm not sure who introduced the idea of imposter syndrome, but it's an elegant term for the tension caused by a disconnect between the perceived and the experiencing self. Classic imposter syndrome is a kind of anticonfidence—a fear of being found out for the flawed and inadequate person we all know (or fear) ourselves to be. In life, it sounds like: "How could someone so wonderful love a person like me? They'll run screaming once they discover the truth." At work, it's the niggling whisper that we don't deserve our successes, aren't qualified for our roles, and will eventually be exposed, humiliated, and sent home in disgrace. With this kind of imposter syndrome, the perception others have of us is right, and the experience we have is misleading. It's a garbage syndrome we dump on ourselves. It's one that needs to be junked and taken down to the dump.

In reverse imposter syndrome, the experiencing self is right, and the perception is wrong. It's what happens when you know the version of yourself other people see—the version you've crafted to be acceptable to those people—isn't who you are. It's less than and inferior to the truth of who you are. It's a syndrome of incongruence, not inadequacy, and it forms at the fault lines of the breakdown.

THE BREAKDOWN WAKE-UP

With apologies to Donald Rumsfeld, perhaps what's most dangerous about human psychology is the number and power of unknown unknowns—emotions, thoughts, and points of pain that exist beneath the level of our awareness like sharks of the soul. Sometimes you catch a glimpse of fin, but for the most part, our minds are the blonde from the Jaws poster, swimming along the surface, cheerfully oblivious to the rising danger. Maybe it's evolutionarily adaptive; maybe if we had clearer insight into our more oceanic urges, we'd be unfit to live in the social groups we need to survive. There are, after all, no schools of sharks.

When we're aware of a problem in our lives, we can usually take actions or make plans to change or mitigate it. It's the problems we don't know we have that are the scariest. Because it's the suppressed or chronic dissatisfactions building up behind the scenes that can take us out, we need to be purposeful about flushing them out of hiding and hauling them into the light.

The first set of signals you'll get that something's starting to fracture are internal, so they're simple to hide. They're uncomfortable to investigate and easy to ignore. They may feel like constriction, a subtle sense of being cramped, crowded, or squeezed, which makes us irritable. They may be draining, slowly, almost (but not entirely) imperceptibly, sucking away pleasure, increasing inertia, and dragging you down. You may feel tired and find that life persistently seems too difficult to wrestle with. An incipient breakdown may feel like you're functioning at half power, handicapped by your mask, and unable to perform the way you once did, or like you're going through life with one hand tied behind your back (and stabbing you).

You may start taking less care with the way you dress because it's no longer a form of self-expression. You may find yourself constantly checking the time, consistently disappointed by how little has passed since you last allowed yourself to look. You take less pride in a job well done and do fewer jobs well. You aren't bothered much by your underperformance. Every day starts to feel like the ones before and those to come, and you move through them with less variation than you get in McDonald's burgers. Which don't even taste good anymore.

You're psychologically hangry at home—unpredictably and irrationally short-tempered—with the people you love. You start spending less time with them, which is, increasingly, how they like it. At your soul-sucking workplace, you keep it under better control. Still, everyone there is in the same frustrated, prickly state. You all lurch around the office physically numb and emotionally hangry, suffering your individual, special form of corporate mental illness. You wonder if it's all that distinguishes you from each other.

SPOTTING THE SIGNS

Some very tuned-in people with a practice of regularly scanning for these circling, emotional fins can spot these fault lines before the buildings start to shake, but often, the earliest tremors are visible from the outside before we can see them ourselves. If your friends start to mention having not seen you for a while, if your spouse is asking if you're getting enough sleep, if your running shoes or gardening gloves, your piano, chessboard, or woodshop is gathering dust, if your kids say they miss you, if whenever anyone asks if you're *really* okay, it irritates you, your life is calling you to pause and reflect. If you don't listen, it will force you.

Maybe you're reading this and asking yourself these questions. Maybe you know the answer because you're already in the shark's mouth or under the collapsed debris. Whether you're just starting to see the cracks or have already broken open, the path of repair and recovery are the same. The energy to start taking them comes from exactly where you are precisely because it's where you don't want to be.

Better is always possible. As long as you're breathing, you have an opportunity to improve. If you're thinking: "My job sucks, but that's life" or "It's not very good, but it's as good as it gets," I declare shenanigans and nonsense! I challenge you to look up from the rock bottom to the blue-sky possibilities. The good news is that the worse things are now, the more room there is for BETTER. We'll get there together.

If you're not all the way down yet, but the sharks are circling, let's get you out of the water. Yes, it's scary. I get that. You're in pain. I get that too. But you're not the first, you're not the last, and you're not alone. You don't have to stay where you are.

With apologies to AA, the first step of fracturing your mask is admitting you're wearing one. Stop pretending that rictus mess is your face.

UNMASKED AND BROKEN

On the kitchen floor, in a puddle of tears and snot, I couldn't keep pretending I was okay. I wasn't and hadn't been for a while. But I'd kept (or tried to keep) all of my not-okay-ness hidden. I couldn't anymore, at least not from myself. And that, it turns out, was a good thing, although I wouldn't have believed it at the time. I was in pieces.

I wasn't "teary-eyed" or "weeping." We're talking about that kind of ugly cry that isn't something you do; it does to you. The kind that turns anyone around you into a mommy who just wants to wrap you up and say, "It's okay, baby. It's okay."

If you asked me to explain what happened next, I couldn't tell you. It was an act of God. I don't think I could have lifted myself up, but in a moment of clarity, I got to my feet. I walked into the bathroom. I stood with my hands gripping the sink edge, and I looked into the mirror. It wasn't pretty. I didn't recognize the man looking back at me, but I knew what I saw was real—you can't fake that kind of ugly. I was a wreck, but somehow, despite that, for the first time in a long time, it was okay. I had a conversation with myself, and I landed on a concept that changed everything for me—the three steps I'm writing this book to share.

Give Yourself a Break

When the mask fractures, the pain is there to prod you out of rock bottom. It can be weirdly tempting to set up camp in that terrible place just because it's where you ended up. It looks like the end of the road. It tastes like failure.

It is, but you aren't.

Where you are isn't who you are. You were at your job, right? And it wasn't who you were. The fact is, you gave it your best shot. You did the best that you could possibly do and you're exactly where you're supposed to be based on your knowledge, resources, and maturity, even if you don't like it and don't want to stay.

Do You Know Better?

> *"When you know better, you do better."*
>
> —MAYA ANGELOU

What you know and what you believe are based on everything you've learned directly and indirectly. You've collected knowledge throughout your life from people who've taught you explicitly and by example. You watched what your parents did and said. You learned things at school and picked them up from TV, your friends, and the world around you. But life can still present you with things you simply don't know how to handle. We all make mistakes and no one can make a good decision with bad information. In fact, it's practically impossible to make good decisions without knowing what a good (or at least a bad) decision looks like.

If you've drunk yourself onto the kitchen floor, you probably knew better. I hadn't, and I didn't. I'd put on the corporate mask not knowing what it would do to me. It really did seem like the right move at the time given what I knew. If you didn't know better, you need to learn more.

But what if you did know better and it all broke down anyway?

Do You Have What You Need?

If you have the knowledge you need, do you have the resources you need to apply what you know? Knowing how to drive isn't much help if you don't have access to a car. Sometimes we know exactly what we need to do, but we don't have the money or the time, the equipment or the relationships. You don't have to own these things; you just need access to them. If you know what you need to do but don't have access to the resources you need, then the road ahead is clear. Do whatever it takes to get what you need to do what you know you need to do. But if you have the knowledge and the resources, there's one more thing you may be lacking.

Will You Do What It Takes?

If you know what you need to do and have the resources to do it, but you simply aren't getting started, if you're choosing to do something else or to do nothing at all, fear, shame, and pain are probably why. Maturity is the willingness, ability, *and* discipline to do what needs to be done when it needs to be done. Without maturity, we can't make the optimal choice. With it, we do.

Every decision in life passes through the three filters of knowledge, resources, and maturity. The action that results is the best we can take with what's left. You can think of them as choke points in a pipe. You're doing the best you can. If it's not good enough, it's because better options were lost to what you didn't know, couldn't get access to, or lacked the maturity to overcome. Life gets very, very hard when your sea of possibilities gets choked down to a trickle. You can open that pipe back up. You just need the right tools.

ACCEPTANCE—A ROTO-ROOTER FOR THE SOUL

Staring back into the bloated, tear-drenched face of the man looking at me from over the bathroom sink, I didn't turn away. I didn't have to accept that mess as my future, but I had to stop pretending it didn't exist. "Okay," I told it. "There you are."

Maybe it was because I was looking at my reflection, maybe God was in the room, but I had enough sense of separation from my reflection to feel compassion for the suffering I saw in the face looking back at me. I didn't judge it. I didn't tell that man he was a failure and a disappointment. I didn't ask him how he thought he deserved to feel so wretched with his loving parents and Ivy League education. I responded to him the way any decent person responds to the suffering of others. I said, "I love you."

I say the same to you now. I love you. No matter what happened, you're okay. Despite the mistakes, failures, and rejections, you're okay. I accept you exactly as you are. You did the best you could.

Do you want to argue with me? Are you thinking, *Jeff, you don't know me*, or that where you are and how you're feeling really, truly isn't okay? That's okay too. It's okay for you to be at the lowest point of your life. It's okay for you to feel like you don't deserve compassion. It's okay to think you're the exception—the one person God doesn't love. Whatever you're feeling or thinking, there you are. Look in the mirror, and say it out loud. "Here I am."

Now what?

Keep looking. There you are; you can't deny that, right? There's a face in the mirror, isn't there? Don't turn away. Whatever fear, shame, anger, or scorn you feel for that face or this exercise, tolerate it. Maybe it's a tear-stained face. Maybe it's a suspicious one. Maybe it's one you're judging as too fat or too old, too something or not enough something else. It's still there. Keep looking at it until the feelings settle down. Maybe you'll get a little bored. That's okay.

You may start thinking this whole exercise is stupid. That's okay too. Keep looking. There you are. Stay there until you can get to: "Okay, yeah. Fine. There I am. There's a face in the mirror. That's how mirrors work, Jeff."

That's all I mean by acceptance. You don't have to love that face or accept the person. You don't have to say, "I love you" or even "You're okay." Acceptance is just about acknowledging reality—not that it's okay, just that it's there. There's a face in the mirror. It's you.

When you know that's true, you're grounded in the moment, in reality. You're out of the swirl of judgment and shame, condemnation and guilt, fear and anger. You're just there. There you are.

That feels better, right? BETTER is possible.

I know I got very lucky or very blessed in that moment I stood there, compassion waking up in me. "There you are" became "Who are you?" At the time, the question had the same slight feeling of dislocation, almost dissociation, that "Who are you, guy in the mirror?" and "Who am I standing here looking at you?" weren't quite the same question.

And I started getting curious about it. *Who am I?* With the acceptance and the curiosity, I felt a rising sense of inspiration. I knew what I needed to do.

There were three steps I needed to take. Taking them wasn't going to be fast or necessarily easy, and once I had taken them, I knew the process they initiated would be one I'd engage in the rest of my life. But at least I wasn't miserable or hopeless anymore. I was excited to get started.

Are your masks fracturing you, or are they starting to crack?

UNMASKING YOUR TRUTH

When you stop hiding who you are and pretending you're okay when you're not, you have to finally confront the feelings and needs you've been ignoring. When you've given up the hand-me-down dream and woken up from the corporate nightmare, you can find yourself in a pretty bleak place. It's not your fault. You did the best you could, given what you knew, the resources you had, and the maturity level you'd attained.

You're where you need to be—wherever that is. But you don't have to stay. **BETTER** is possible. We'll get there together.

Sobbing on the kitchen floor, staring into the bathroom mirror, I wasn't alone. I couldn't have moved from despair and self-loathing to compassion and insight so quickly on my own. God was there with me, and I'm grateful every day. I also recognize how much longer it would have taken me to get to a life I genuinely love living if I'd had to find the path on my own. To be honest, I fear I might have been like so many people who never get there. But thankfully, I discovered a way out, and I want to share it with you. The three steps I'm going to teach you next aren't just another pair of tablets carried down from Mount Sinai. They're also the steps I walked on my way back from hell.

If you've felt the shift out of your head and into reality—if you've experienced even a moment of recognition that you are here, now, where you are—you're living in the process. Maybe you're not inspired by it yet. Maybe you don't really believe that better is possible. That's okay. I'll talk you through each step and share my experience on the path.

Ready? We'll start with Step 1, talking about identity.

Chapter 4

STEP 1:
WHO AM I?

I'm a first-generation college graduate on my dad's side. He grew up as one of four kids raised by a single mother who worked as many as three jobs just to keep the worst scenarios at bay. Dad started working at fourteen, and even though he did a semester at a junior college, when he found a job making good money, he took it and held on tight.

On my mom's side of the family, you have to go back three generations to find the first college graduate and more than I can track to find the first of what today would be called an entrepreneur or small business owner—the kind of people who ran a trucking company, owned a junkyard or delivered the milk. Even the ones who worked for someone had a side hustle they worked for themselves.

I inherited a strong work ethic from both parents and with it, the absolute faith that putting in the hours and effort yields rewards. They taught that gospel in what they said and how they lived, and I had firsthand proof it was true by the time I was in high school. I was blessed with a certain amount of musical talent, and I loved music, but I spent tons of time in the woodshed (that means practicing if you don't speak Musician).

My parents taught me the truest version of the American dream—that with hard work and the right education, I could do anything I wanted to do and be whatever I wanted to be. In fact, to shield me from the industrial dream and protect me from the corporate machine, they went to the (I thought extreme) length of prohibiting me from working at McDonald's or the local movie theater.

They gave me one reason (they wanted me to focus on school), but I suspect they had another. I think that, deliberately or not, they were training me to be enterprising. They forbid me from being a part of someone else's business. I had no choice but to create my own value streams.

My parents' marriage (like most, I suppose) was a layer cake of harmony and tension. They were in absolute agreement about the virtue and value of working hard, but they held different attitudes about the relationship between work, freedom, and stability. I internalized both Mom's "spread your wings and fly" and Dad's "keep your feet on the ground and a roof over your head" philosophies.

These two mindsets weren't irreconcilably different, but they weren't completely congruent, and the difference created friction I didn't realize was holding me back. When it became clear that there wasn't room at my work for the breadth of their span, I clipped my wings. It was an unwitting compromise between my mother's answer and my dad's. It was 50 percent each of them and 0 percent me.

I'd been working hard and performing well at my job, and when that failed to earn me the recognition and rewards I'd expected, I started working hard at being the company man. When that much effort and sacrifice still failed to deliver, part of what broke me was the idea that my parents' faith in hard work had let me down. I didn't recognize that at the time. Looking at my face in the bathroom mirror, I couldn't see the hybrid I'd made, only that whoever was looking back at me wasn't who I wanted to be. And I started asking why.

You have to be you before you can be a BETTER you. Until you can acknowledge the past and understand your mistakes and failures, you can't let them go and move forward with your wins and wisdom.

From here on out, this book will be a collaboration between us—writer and reader, you and me. I'll ask you a lot of questions, and the more thought you put into answering them, the more quickly you'll move toward BETTER. The questions in this chapter are designed to help you gain insights into the compromises you may have made under the influence of your parents' ideals and to articulate your own, to understand where you came from, what you brought with you, and what you might choose to let go. I encourage you to write down your answers and to take notes on what you learn about yourself.

Nobody knows your story better than you do, and no path is one-size-fits-all. Your answers will originate in your past, resolve your present, and activate your future. They will be uniquely yours, but the questions are universal. When we're done, you'll have more insight into who you are.

WHO I AM

I think you probably know me pretty well by now. I hope so. I've shared as much of my life story with you as I have because I want you to know you have a friend on this journey you're on and that I've walked the path before you.

Who I am now is not who I was when I became a company man or when I had my ugly cry. The fact that you're reading this book is a testament to that. This amount of candor isn't possible from behind a mask. I lived the steps and worked through the questions. I figured out who I was and who I wanted to be, and then I went to work becoming that guy.

Today I know my purpose, and I live it daily (even though no two days in a row look alike). Whether I'm speaking on stages across the country, helping entrepreneurs raise hundreds of thousands of dollars, performing in world-renowned jazz venues, or working to revolutionize the way recent college grads land their dream jobs, I still recognize the face in the mirror. And I like who I see—the man I am now and the man I am still becoming.

My purpose is to help others live a life worth remembering. It's a vision for my life (and for a better world) based on the feeling that accompanies the best moments of our lives. In those peak moments, knowing they won't, can't, and shouldn't last, there's a desire to immortalize it. We take a photo, make a journal entry, or simply call the moment out to the person we're lucky enough to be sharing it with. Everything I do now is about helping people create more moments they want to remember. It's become my life's tagline: Creating Lives Worth Remembering.

I was lucky enough to share the meta-moment of recognizing my purpose (and wanting to remember the importance *of wanting to remember the most important moments*) with my wife. We were in the living room together, and I still remember turning to her and saying, "Wife, I've figured it out!"

But my life purpose and tagline didn't drop out of the sky. I'd been thinking about it for a while, looking back over everything I'd done—in entertainment and entrepreneurship, mentoring and marketing—and turning them around in my head like a mental Rubik's Cube. That night in the living room, it all finally clicked into place.

The moment was giddy and profound, but it was a long time coming, and it all started with asking why and then following my own tracks, my people, and the knowledge, resources, and maturity that filtered my choices. It's time for you to do the same.

FOLLOW YOUR WHYS

There's a popular strategic technique of following the cause-and-effect train back up its tracks a distance of five whys to the root cause of whatever's showing up in your life. Without consciously calling on it as a technique, I started asking myself a series of critical *whys*. Why was I so empty and angry? The answer was easy: I hated my job. The next why was a little harder to see and much harder to look at.

Why did I hate my job? It was a great job. If you'd asked me where I wanted to work and what I wanted to be doing there, my answer would have mostly matched my job description. Still, I was miserable. *Why?* I hated my job because I hated my life. *Why?* Because it felt divided into buckets with no one place where I could be my whole self. *Why?*

There were two ways to answer that fifth why. The first is obvious—I was wearing a mask at work because my employer had asked me to put one on, *and I'd agreed to do so.* My job had made the success I sought contingent on being two people. There was Job Jeff, and then there was Jazz Jeff—the guy I had to leave at home when I went into the office. So that's what I did.

The deeper answer to why I felt so estranged from myself required looking back a generation or even two. I couldn't be my whole self because I couldn't reconcile my mother's freedom with my father's stability. I'd chosen to sacrifice one in the name of the other. It's almost as if there was both a dreamer and a planner within me, and I couldn't be two people.

YOUR TURN

What in your life (or missing from it) is causing you the most pain? Write it as an "I am" statement. For me, it was anger. (I am angry all the time). Next, ask yourself why you are the way you are. (Why am I angry?) Then ask yourself the why behind that. Keep going. Get at least five whys deep. You'll know you're done when you give yourself an answer you didn't know.

FOLLOW YOUR TRACKS

What do you see as your three greatest failures? Your three biggest successes? Understanding what they are and what caused them can shed more light on who you are. You can follow your tracks from the present back to the past or from the past up to the present.

What choices did you make (or neglect to make) that shaped the most impactful events of your life? Are there formative events in which you had no choices to make? Sometimes, God, your parents, a natural disaster, or a random stranger can keep you from the most fundamental freedom of self-determination. If so, in some way or another, you were enslaved. This event may have caused you to do things, but you didn't cause the event.

The difference here is subtle but essential. When you're looking for causes, there are really only two kinds: things you did (or didn't do) and things that were done (or not done) to you. When you're trying to reconcile things that happened to you, going backward isn't about you. It's not your fault *that* it happened but understanding *why* it did can still be revealing.

It's what we did in Chapter 1. I didn't cause my promotion not to come through. The higher-ups at my company held a false belief that kept me from advancement. I chose to put on a mask at work as a result, but I didn't choose the cause. Tracking it led us back up the Good Job Pipeline to its origin in the Industrial Revolution. Understanding the source of the myth I was living inside allowed me to get outside of it and decide to choose something new.

People who track their current "I am" back to some kind of abuse or neglect can find that, while it doesn't excuse the offense, understanding the motivations or circumstances behind what happened helps them let go of some of the anger, guilt, resentment or shame they've been carrying. Working with a professional therapist can be a great help.

.

YOUR TURN

Are there things that happened in your life that you didn't have any hand in causing? Work five whys in each direction. First, what did you choose (consciously or unconsciously) to do in response, and what were the results? Keep going forward in time until you land at a present "I am." Second, look at the event itself. Why did it happen? Keep going back in time until you reach a level where emotional distance is possible. Enlist help if you need to.

When you follow your tracks back to their origin, they're almost always positive or value-neutral. I tracked mine to an understanding that I chose to sell some of my freedom without realizing the real cost and without questioning whether or not that was the only option. Did the younger me have to choose between them? No. They aren't actually mutually exclusive. (I'm living proof!) But I have nothing but love for the younger man who didn't know any better. That guy did what he thought was right.

No matter how many crates of guilt or shame you're carrying, when you track back to the moment you picked each one up, I think you'll see you either had a good reason or shouldered it without deliberate thought. Once you identify the moment you picked them up, you can put them down with compassion and love.

YOUR TURN

What's keeping you from loving your entire self? Make a list. Track it back
(or forward) until you understand why you did what you did. Can you
accept the person you were for doing what you did at the maturity level,
resources, and knowledge you had at the time? If not, ask yourself
another why or five until you can.

FOLLOW YOUR PEOPLE

In 2009, my mom became gravely ill. We weren't sure she would survive, and I took a leave of absence from my job to become her full-time
caregiver. When I ran out of vacation time, I took a freelance job
because it gave me more flexibility to be there for Mom. As it turned
out, the freelance job was a substantial pay increase. More money.
More flexibility. It ended up allowing me to experience freedom and
prosperity in ways I never knew existed outside of the traditional,
"secure" path.

Maybe you took a job and put on a mask because taking care of your
kids was the most important thing in the world to you. Maybe you
made a choice (conscious or otherwise) to sacrifice anything for
your children, including your true self. Was it necessary, or did some
unquestioned belief about what it means to be a good parent prompt

you to give up your unique passions, gifts, and skills simply to prove your love?

If the sacrifice was necessary once, is it still? If you're still in a job you hate once your kids are out of college and supporting themselves, there's something beyond parental love going on.

My dad saw how hard, long, and thanklessly his mother worked to take care of her family. I'm sure a determination never to be that hard up for work was part of the reason he clung so fiercely to the first good job he got.

Do you have a spouse or longtime partner? Are you working to support their standard of living or compete with their career? Is your job where you hide out when you don't want to go home? Does your partner have opinions or anxieties about your professional choices? How heavy a thumb do they put on that scale?

Whether or not you have children or a significant other, think about your parents. How many of your choices were made to please or placate them? Have you been trying to prove your worth or earn their love? Did you simply follow the career path they picked out for you?

We are all people, and people are where we all come from. Understanding the ones who've come before you and the ones who've joined you along the way can help you get a clearer picture of your own true, naked face and teach you who you are by learning where you came from.

YOUR TURN

Who are the people who mean the most to you?

Why do they matter?

How long have they been a part of your life?

How do they connect to this moment where you are right now?

FOLLOW YOUR FILTERS

In the last chapter, I said you're always exactly where you're supposed to be, having arrived (as we always do) on a path made of choices. Your available choices are filtered by what you know, the resources you have, and your level of maturity. Looking back across your personal and family history, can you see gaps in knowledge, resources, or maturity that closed down certain paths to you? Conversely, what stepping stones can you leverage to skip a few steps ahead? Because these filters constrain your choices, they're a huge part of who you are. Let's take an inventory!

Knowledge

Knowledge is everything you've learned, read, or experienced. It's anything about which you can say "I know that." It includes skills you've mastered, insights you've gained, and observations you've made.

YOUR TURN

In your "how many years" on this planet, what have you learned?

What skills have you picked up?

List any areas where you are more knowledgeable than the average bear.

Do you have an advanced or specialized degree?

Do you speak more than one language?

Have you had unusual experiences or gone places few of your peers have gone?

Resources

Knowledge is rarely enough on its own. Executing on what you know almost always requires access to some additional resources, even if they're just time and energy. More often, you'll need some equipment or money, tools or collaboration to help you act on what you know. You don't have to own them, but you need access to them.

YOUR TURN

What resources are you missing that, if you had, would enable you to be more of who you are?

What absorbs your attention and your cash?

How deep are your pockets of time, energy, and attention?

How rich are you in friendship, family, and love?

Where do you spend your energy, and what replenishes it?

Where does your time go? What takes up the most of your awake, non-work hours?

Which of your time expenditures delivers the best ROI?

Which brings in nothing at all or dips into the negative?

Maturity

Maturity means having the mental and emotional fortitude to make the right decisions—and to consistently act on them. It can be difficult not to compare your interior to someone else's exterior. We all want to be more disciplined, have stronger willpower, and procrastinate less. In fact, the leading indicator of immaturity is the conviction that you're all grown up and done. For our purposes, maturity means the ability to do what you know you need to do and not do what you know you shouldn't. Since it tends to be most evident in its absence, try to measure your maturity level by your outcomes.

YOUR TURN

How many difficult things have you done?

What have you stuck with beyond the point that it was fun?

When have you given up short-term pleasures for long-term gains?

Are you physically fit?

Do you have money in savings?

Do you get your work in on time?

Have you kept a household together—done the laundry and the shopping, made the meals, and taken out the trash?

What obstacles have you pushed through?

What difficult hurdles have you jumped?

WHO ARE YOU?

Once you've answered all of the questions in this chapter, read through your answers. Notice the patterns and themes, the pitfalls and springboards. Then write your personal history for a deeper understanding of your identity (which marketing people would call the foundation of your *brand*).

This is an important exercise because your unexamined past is a heavy ball of regret chained to you by shame. After you've written your story, read it back to yourself—slowly. Accept it, and accept yourself fully without filters or embarrassment, free from regrets and shame. Acknowledging and accepting your mistakes frees you from the weight that's holding you back and grinding you down. When you know who you are and can acknowledge and love (or at least accept) all of the different aspects of yourself, you have a starting point from which you can go almost anywhere.

It's a cliché that life is a journey, but it's overused because it's true. You're not done 'til you're dead. You're not a failure 'til you quit.

You did the best you could. How do I know? Because if you could have done better, you would have.

Chapter 5

STEP 2: WHO DO I WANT TO BE?

In 1994, I was eleven and headed into sixth grade. In Detroit, sixth, seventh, and eighth grades are grouped into a middle school, so leaving fifth grade meant going to a new school. My family lived in a nice enough neighborhood, and the local elementary school had been a great experience for me. Now it was time to get on the bus to a part of town that was—let's say "economically challenged." It wasn't unusual for me to pass as many prostitutes as I had fingers on the way home from school.

I'd skipped a grade, so I was a year younger than most kids in my class, but I had friends and didn't get any trouble from anyone—even the one kid in my class who was a solid three years older than I was. He'd been held back two years, and even had a full beard! (What can I say? Kids do a lot of growing between eleven and fourteen.) This kid had taken up his own kind of junior mask of the thug persona—all aggression and indifference.

He never gave me any trouble, but I'd watched him the way younger kids watch older kids. I knew he was smart—much smarter than his academic performance (or lack thereof) suggested. It was almost the end of the school year before I thought to say anything to him, and honestly, I don't remember what I did say in the end. It was just an observation on my part, but it was something along the lines of, "You know, you can be hard and still get good grades."

I didn't go back to that school for seventh grade. I hadn't had a bad experience, but it wasn't what my parents wanted for me. I transferred to another middle school, moved on to high school and Wharton, then returned to Detroit. Ten years after I left that first middle school, I was reminded of it by a Facebook message from a guy I didn't recognize. In the message, he thanked me for changing his life.

I still appreciate him taking the time to reach out to me because if he hadn't, I would never have heard his story nor captured a critical life lesson along the way. He told me that our conversation had been transformative for him. Turns out, he'd really listened to my words of encouragement and started to excel academically the following school year. He got promoted a year, finished middle school close to on time, and went from there into a technical high school. He graduated, went to college, graduated again, and was in med school at the point when he sent me the message.

I love this story, and not because it makes me look good! It is, I think, less a testament to my eleven-year-old eloquence than to the power of revealed possibility. We don't reach for what we can't see. All that kid needed to completely turn his life around was the idea that he could be who he was *and* be something better.

Having discarded the hand-me-down dream, in this chapter it's time to tailor one of your own. Your aspirational self is a vision seen through multiple lenses that may change over time but which guides and inspires you to reach beyond your grasp and higher than the horse you rode in on.

Discovering and defining who you want to be is an exercise in seeing what isn't yet there. In this chapter, we'll talk about why you need a clear vision of an aspirational self, and I'll take you through the steps of creating one. We'll build a Venn diagram of your overlapping desires and values, your passions, gifts and skills, and the causes, needs, and wants that your vision of the good life and best self need to include.

THE ASPIRATIONAL SELF

If you don't know where you want to go, you'll never get there. I know that sounds a little obvious when you think about it, but most people seem to go through life with only the vaguest idea of what they want their lives to eventually look like. When the hand-me-down dream of "a good job," which is somehow assumed to mean a good life (whatever *that* means), fails to materialize, it's easy to continue drifting in the direction you were initially pushed. This gets you nowhere. Or onto the kitchen floor. The only thing that will get you up and moving again is something even stronger than a dream—a vision.

VISION

Without a vision, life is a series of accidents—happy or otherwise—and while the happy-accident lifestyle makes great TV, it's hard to sustain in reality. The Bible says, "Where there is no vision, the people perish" (Proverbs 29:18). A vision gives you a target and a destination for your life that's clearer and more specific than the dreamy dream reality displaced. A vision puts you back in the driver's seat of your life and activates a powerful GPS.

Without intention, success is just a happy accident.

I want to challenge you to replace the dream you were bottle-fed with one of your own creation. Create a vision for who you want to be, not just so that you can move forward successfully from there, but because by living with intent you will achieve more for yourself and the world we share.

CRAFTING A VISION

A vision is clearer than a dream. It's something you can see, not just imagine. There are no hand-me-down visions. You have to build your own. Building anything requires active effort and, ideally, some kind of blueprint or plan. In short, you need a vision for your vision, a plan for creating your life plan. A clear vision defines what success means to you, lets you know whether you're on the right path and when you've reached that aspirational destination. Your vision becomes the mentor you never had, guiding you along the way to a better future. To build one, you'll create a composite picture of your aspirational self from several layered lenses.

Lens: Desire

Think about the person you want to be ten or fifteen years from now. Try to see your aspirational self as clearly as you can in your mind's eye. Notice what you look like and how it's different from your current appearance. Imagine the typical day in the life of this ideal future you. Notice the morning routines they follow, the kind of clothes they wear, and where (or whether) they go into work. Now imagine a typical weekend and see your aspirational self doing the kind of leisure and restorative activities you want to be a part of your future. Finally, think about the extraordinary days—the birthdays, holidays, and vacations—and visualize what you most want for your future self.

YOUR TURN

Write a description of the person you want to be ten or fifteen years
from now. What does that person look like? What does the ideal future
you sound like? Close your eyes and imagine that person. It's okay if they
look and sound like someone you know. It's okay if they don't. Just try to
get a sense of them there in the room with you. What would role-model
you say to you now?

Lens: Values

When you think about the kind of person you want to be, do certain
traits or characteristics pop into your head? What feels most important
to you? For me, the word "love" just shows up. I want to be loving.

YOUR TURN

Who do you want to be like?

Think about the people you most respect and admire. You don't have to
restrict yourself to people you know or even ones who are alive. Work on
your list for a while. What is it about those people that appeals to you? Maybe

they're loving or accomplished, disciplined or spontaneous, courageous or contemplative, principled, radical, or sensual. Write out your list.

Now, take a hard look at your list. There are traits I admire in others that I don't aspire to in myself. For example, I have a lot of respect for peaceful, calm people, but mellow isn't part of my aspirational self. I'm a high-energy guy; I have no interest in being subdued. Of the attributes and personality traits you've listed, which are the most important to you? Which three to five belong in the description of your aspirational self?

YOUR TURN

What wouldn't you do?

Think of the things you most want to be, do, and have. What would you *not* do to get them? If you wouldn't kill someone for money, you value life. If you wouldn't give up your family for anything, you value family. Write out your list.

Would you sacrifice your health to take that vacation? Would you give up owning a house to be able to travel the world? Would you trade keeping your house clean for an extra two grand a month? Is there anything you'd never do—anything you'd choose death over?

Don't get too far into the calculus of it. You're not Sophie, and you're not actually trying to rank your values or make these trade-offs; you're just filtering for what matters most to you as a lens into who you are and who you want to be.

Now, take a look at the list you've created of the things you value most. Does it feel pretty complete? Can you narrow it down? Now check that list against the list of adjectives from the first question in this section about who you wanted to be like. Does that list align with this one? If you've discovered there's nothing you wouldn't give up to have a wife and kids, family man belongs on your list even if you're single. If adventurous is on your list, but you've realized you wouldn't give up much to travel the world, your aspirational self may be more domestic than you thought. Part of shaking off the hand-me-down dream is separating the things we believe we are supposed to want from those we actually do.

Lens: Money

When searching for a vision of a future that's exciting and aspirational, you need not a new lens, but rather the absence of one so ubiquitous that seeing without it can be tricky. We have such trouble imagining what work means without money that it's easier to think about having all the money you need than it is to wrap your head around not needing money.

Imagine you've won the lottery or, if that seems too crazy, pretend you started a company, worked super hard for eight years, and sold it for billions. Do whatever it takes to get your rational, doubting mind to go with the exercise. With absolutely no need to worry about price tags ever again, what would you do?

I'm guessing celebrate, travel, and sleep, in that order (or another one depending on how exhausted you're imagining you are). Then what?

YOUR TURN

With more money than you could spend and all the time in the world, once everything settles down, leaving you with the freedom to decide what your new normal will look like, what would you put on your to-do list? What would you do if money wasn't an object?

This can be a surprisingly difficult question to answer, and four traps are way too easy to fall into. You can't see as much from the bottom of a hole. This exercise is all about creating as broad an aspirational field as you can conceive. Real freedom can be hard to imagine. Try. Make a list. And watch out for traps.

The Work-or-Play Trap

Think about the things that fill you up, that you love doing just for the sake of doing them. Try not to get caught up in the difference between "work" and "play." You can work very hard at playing a sport or an instrument. If you're like most people, a more important distinction is whether or not progress is possible. Doing easy things can make you happy, but only challenging things keep you fulfilled. It's the difference between watching a sport and being out on the field with your friends.

YOUR TURN

What are your hobbies?

What do you do right now for free?

When you were a kid, what kind of things did you choose to do with your time?

What kind of things do you see other people doing and think: It would be nice to _____?

The Realism Trap

Many of us were encouraged to stop pursuing things we loved because there was "no future" in them. Don't fall into the "it's not realistic" trap. We'll get there, I promise. But for right now, try not to limit your vision to what you've already seen. If you love to dance, but you have a bum ankle, being a professional ballerina might be unrealistic. That doesn't matter right now. It's exactly those things you'd do no matter what that we're looking for here. If space travel fascinates and inspires you, if you really want to be an astronaut, that's great! Don't tell me you're too old or too anything else to do any of the things that make you feel alive. Add them to your list.

The Forever Trap

If you find yourself thinking of things you'd like to try but aren't sure you'd want to do forever, put them on your list. Your dream can change. In fact, it probably will. That's not failure, and it doesn't mean it wasn't your true vision of your ideal future or your best self.

Part of the false dream we've been sold is the One True Career narrative. You go to college, pick a major, get a job in that field, and work in it until you retire. This narrative is great for employers, but that doesn't mean it has to be right for you. Likewise, what you put on your list doesn't have to be what you want to always be doing. Doing one single thing eight hours a day, five days a week, fifty weeks a year probably isn't *your* dream. It's a hand-me-down.

The Judgment Trap

Unless your dream is to hurt innocent people (in which case, see a therapist, please!), don't let anyone tell you your dream isn't okay. Maybe you really love to beat the snot out of folks, and a future in the MMA ring lights you up inside. More power to you. (Just remind me not to piss you off.)

Try to keep what you create in your imagination free of any kind of right-or-wrong, good-or-bad judgments. It's okay if it's selfish and doesn't help anyone but you. If it's something you find valuable, it doesn't matter if no one else benefits or sees its utility. We're not concerned with that yet. For the moment, just keep an open mind about what brings you joy, what feeds your soul and fills your tank.

When you know what you'd do if money were no object, you know what you're passionate about. Passion is great!

Lens: Passions, Gifts, and Skills

If a passion is anything you love doing, gifts are the things that naturally come easily to you, and skills are things you've worked to get good at. Looking through the money lens above, you probably got a good view of what you love doing, but often passions, gifts, and skills overlap. Music, for me, is all three.

I've always loved music. When I started playing, it came easily to me, and I practiced hard and got better. I'd do it for free (though I'm happy to collect a handsome fee for it). I was also a talented athlete and practiced enough to be skillful. I enjoyed it, sure, but I could imagine a happy life that didn't involve playing a sport. A life without music wouldn't be life. I don't think it'd even be possible.

Sometimes, your strongest gifts come so naturally that they're almost invisible. If you've ever heard yourself say, "Anyone can (fill in the blank: dance, sing, do math, cook)," it's a good indication that you have a gift in that area because—trust me—there's nothing everyone can do well.

YOUR TURN

What are your passions, gifts, and skills?

What do you simply love doing for its own sake?

What were you praised for when you were a kid, beyond the compliments your parents gave you? (Parental praise is often a better picture of what they valued than of who you were.)

What subjects did you get good grades in?

What did teachers call out about you?

> Who were you to your peers?
>
> Were you the smart one, the funny one, the sensitive one, the one who'd try anything twice?

Ask other people what they think you're good at, and you'll probably be surprised at their answers. I knew a guy who was exceptionally good at connecting people from his different friend and work groups. It came so naturally to him, he had no idea he was doing it until someone pointed it out. Once he was aware of his ability, he started doing it more deliberately and several creative collaborations, job offers, and at least two marriages came out of it. And counting!

If you're not comfortable directly asking people about what you're exceptionally good at, think about the things people ask you to do—and I'm not talking about the laundry! In what areas do people ask for your help or your advice? For example, are you the guy everyone asks for dating tips or car repair help? Are you the one in your family with the fashion sense or the hot travel tips? Do all your friends come to you when they want new restaurant recommendations or when they can't figure out how to lose weight?

Passion and ability go together, especially when we're young. If you were naturally good at sports and got positive feedback for performing well, you might have enjoyed the praise enough to keep going to practice, where you got better and earned more praise—even if you didn't really enjoy the sport.

> ## YOUR TURN
>
> Were there things you loved doing when you were young that you weren't good at but still loved?
>
> Were there things your parents or friends teased you about doing, but you did anyway because they were just too much fun to give up?

In the same way that it can be hard to know what comes naturally to you because it comes so naturally that you don't even notice it, it's easy to overlook your gifts in your future vision. I believe that gifts are well-named—they're abilities given to us by God, and putting them to good use is the closest we can get to writing a thank-you note. If your gifts don't have a place in your vision of your ideal future, it's worth taking another look to see where they might fit.

Lens: People

You were not put on this planet to be alone. In addition to the things you want to do, your vision of your future self needs to include the person or people you'll be spending your time with. The people lens has three filters: "called to," "have to," and "want to." Sometimes—often, if you're lucky—these groups overlap, and the people you feel called to be with, those you have to be around and those whose company you enjoy, are the same. Often, there's a bit of a gap. There are bosses or family members you can't escape, totally optional friends or mentors you'd love to have more of in your life, and then there are those folks with whom you share a magnetic pull you wouldn't change if you could, and you can't.

YOUR TURN

Looking back over your life, who are the people (both specific individuals and the types of personalities or professions) who seem to have been drawn to you or toward whom you gravitated?

I have a friend who's called to work with young children. The minute any child under four years old walks into the room, she lights up. Five minutes later, she's sitting on the floor, absorbed in play or nurturing, regardless of her original plans for the evening or the white pants never meant for getting down and dirty with four-year-olds. She's aware of this tendency in herself, but until we talked about it, kids (neither her own nor other people's) weren't part of her future vision. I'm not saying she has to be a parent, but if at least occasional interaction with her nieces and nephews or Sunday school kids aren't a part of her life, she's going to feel like something is missing.

Sometimes, the people component is about the effect you have on them, which is often also tied to a gift. If you love to make people laugh, if coaching or tutoring is rewarding to you, or if you're the person everyone turns to for parenting advice, your impact on others needs to be part of your people plan. For me, it's creating memorable moments for others—something I discovered working through this exercise on my own.

Lens: Causes

If you can't stand the idea of kids without a loving adult in their lives, or if the plight of abandoned animals creates such powerful feelings that you can barely think about them, if you simply can't believe that slavery and human trafficking still exist, or if you simply have to see a world where basic healthcare is a human right, your powerful emotional response is a signpost.

YOUR TURN

Is there something in the world that sets you on fire?

Any cause that resonates with you strongly needs to be a part of your future. I'm not saying you have to devote yourself to it full-time, but passionate outrage or longing is too rich a source of energy and meaning not to include in your vision.

If you don't have a cause that lights a fire in you, that's fine. But if you do, don't ignore it because you don't want to give up your comfortable lifestyle to become a saint.

The All-or-Nothing Trap

I have a friend whose young daughter once answered the inevitable "What do you want to be when you grow up?" question with this response: "A doctor, a baseballer, and a red dump truck."

We're still not exactly sure what the kid meant, but the diversity embedded in her answer is significant. In another year or two, her answer will likely narrow to something like "soccer player." The idea that we can be only one thing is at the core of why my boss's boss didn't think I was serious about my work even though I was, and performed better than other people with less going on to boot. People who play baseball and drive trucks are more than capable of being doctors. (I can't help you with *being* a truck.)

Lens: What You Need

As you work through this and the lenses that follow, don't eliminate something because you wouldn't want it to be your full-time job or to do it to the exclusion of everything else. Sure, dancing for the New York City Ballet might require you to do very little beyond practice, sleep, and not eat, but you can take a once-a-week barre class and lead a happier life as a nurse than if you simply decided you no longer want to dance.

But let's not forget about the moolah! Money isn't really optional. Navigating the world requires financial resources, and while you can learn a lot about what you truly love by imagining what you'd do if money wasn't an object, it *is* an object—an important one. I'm fairly sure nobody's vision of an ideal future would be complete without it. Unlike the previous parts of this exercise, knowing how much money you want is easy—we all want all the money. The critical question here isn't about want, though; it's about need.

Ask yourself how much money you need to be satisfied. Not how much you need to survive, or how much you need to have everything you want, but how much you need for the lack of money not to detract from your enjoyment of life.

Let's take a simple inventory: for how many people, in addition to yourself, are you financially responsible or partially responsible? If your ideal future vision includes a spouse and/or children you don't currently have, figure them into the equation.

YOUR TURN

How much money do you need to remove money from your list of anxieties?

How much money do you need to take appropriate care of yourself and the people for whom you are responsible?

This book isn't designed to help you plan your financial life. If you want to qualify your numbers for this exercise, please see a financial planner or check out one of Dave Ramsey's excellent books.

Lens: What You Want

Once you have a ballpark sense of what it would take to be fully functional financially, with a reasonable place to live, enough good-quality food to eat, a reliable and safe way of getting where you need to go, no consumer debt, and a savings buffer, ask yourself what you want that goes beyond what you need.

We're looking for a benchmark number, not the bare minimum you can survive on or the maximum you could find a way to spend. There are purchases that you need, ones you want, and ones that would be nice to have. Stick to the first two.

YOUR TURN

What would go on a "Have List" of everything you'd like to have?

What do you (or would you like to) spend money on that adds value to your life?

Would life simply not be as enjoyable if you couldn't go out to eat someplace nicer than Subway once a month?

Would a luxury SUV simply make you happy each time you got behind the wheel?

Does a life without travel feel like less of a life?

YOUR TURN: OVERLAPPING THE LENSES

Draw five intersecting circles on a piece of paper. You're going to title the circles as follows:

1. Passions

2. Gifts

3. Skills

4. People

5. Purpose

Start populating each of these circles with the relevant information from the lists you've made. When something shows up in more than one area, write it in the overlapping oval.

For me, for example, music is a passion, a gift, and a skill. Musicians are on my list of my people, and because music is one of the ways I contribute to the making of memorable experiences for others, music goes in the overlap of all five circles.

When you're done, take a look at the middle of your Venn diagram. The self you aspire to doesn't have to live right in the middle of your Venn diagram. Instead, think of these areas of overlap as gravity sinks. Your life will be pulled in these directions, and the less friction that tug encounters, the smoother your life is likely to be.

What's critical isn't trying to optimize for circle density, but having a visual representation of how integrated you actually already are. It's very easy for our dreams to feel siloed by life, but those boundaries are frequently much more arbitrary than they may look at first. Get creative. A love for medicine and trucks might be satisfied by working as an EMT. The more overlaps, the more power you'll have. You don't have to build a life at the center of the diagram, but there is a euphoria there, and you want to make sure you can at least visit it regularly.

Why wouldn't you live in the center of the circles full-time? Take a look at your Have List. Unless you're exceptionally lucky, there may very well be experiences and possessions you want to have that living at the intersection of your passions, gifts, skills, people, and purposes won't supply. You may find that some things on your Have List seem less appealing now, and it would be easy to give some up to spend more time in the center of your diagram. Sure, yearly trips to Bali might be great to have, but maybe you'd rather spend less time vacationing if you got to spend more time doing what you'd do for free with the people you love to be with, exercising your gifts, and building your skills. Also, remember that nothing says vacation can't mean taking a month off work to star in your community theater's production of *Hamlet*.

WHO DO YOU WANT TO BE?

Creating a vision of your aspirational self is a powerful exercise in individual dream creation that can identify and propel you toward your most important goals by focusing on the activities, traits, and values that matter most to you.

Your aspirational self, once envisioned, becomes the mentor you never had and widens your vision of what's possible, like my comment to the middle school bully unwittingly did. He took the quickest sketch of a better version of himself—one that added performing well in school—and used it to alter his life trajectory. Think how much power powerful your thoughtfully constructed aspirational self will be! With that in mind:

YOUR TURN

Write a letter introducing your aspirational self to me.

Write a letter from your aspirational self to who you are today.
Start with the words, "Thank you."

It's incredibly cliché, but life really is a journey. You don't arrive 'til you die. The path between who you are and the future, aspirational you is made of choices—choices you can make either deliberately or by default. The more ownership you take of your choices, the more ownership you have of your future and your life. The path made of choices is the unfolding road of becoming. In the next chapter, you'll take the wheel and start driving!

Chapter 6

STEP 3:
WHO AM I BECOMING?

Let's go back to where we left me—the bathroom sink. The process I've outlined in the previous two chapters is one I developed in the months after my breakdown, but I lived through the highlights reel as I stood there, and what I saw gave me confidence in the process and hope that sustained me as I did the work I've just outlined for you. In the moment, the condensed version played out like this:

I asked the splotchy, snotty face in the mirror who it was. I said it out loud—*Who am I? Who do I want to be?*

I didn't really know the answers, but I knew their inverse. *Not this.*

The man looking back at me was neither who I was nor who I wanted to be. I knew my choices had brought me to this place and that if I kept doing what I'd been doing, I'd keep moving further away from where I wanted to be. I looked into my own red eyes. *You have to do things differently.*

And I did. I stopped what I'd been doing. I took off my corporate mask because, even if I hadn't figured out who I was yet, I knew this person in the mirror wasn't it. I started working on my answers to the first two "who" questions, inventorying my identity, and envisioning my aspirational self. Then I started becoming who I wanted to be.

It's relatively easy to be bold about your past or have a beautiful dream for the future, but the real power to achieve lives in your becoming.

In Chapter 5, you made an account of your past and developed your present identity. In the previous chapter, you looked into the future to envision your aspirational self. Here, we'll put that self to work in the fleeting but constant moment between the past and the future—the unfolding now.

You'll learn to manage your present in a way that increases your knowledge, resources, and maturity, and makes you the master of your identity and vision. We'll look again at all of the things you found you wanted as you began to articulate your aspirational self and discuss the ordering of being, doing, and having. We'll look at what creates a self and inventory the hand-me-down thoughts, words, and habits you might be happier without. Finally, you'll learn to leverage your aspirational self to differentiate between your reactions and responses to increase your mastery over yourself today and the better self you're becoming for your future.

TRANSFORMATION

For your best to get better, you have to *be* better. Being BETTER (getting better at being) means improving your thoughts, words, and actions in a way that moves you closer to your aspirational self and increases your knowledge, resources, and maturity so that you get more of what you want and hold onto it.

Coming back to the present from the future you've been imagining can feel a bit bumpy. Once you've clearly imagined what's possible and envisioned who you want to be, your present and your present self almost inevitably fall short. While it's still true that you aren't who you want to be at this exact moment, the difference is that now you know where you're headed. The gap between where you are and the ideal future you've imagined isn't empty space—it's a generator. Think of the tension you feel between who you are now and who you want to be in five years as the tension in a wound spring. It's stored energy. It's what powers your becoming.

WHO'S THE MASTER?

We've already talked about slavery and ownership—about whose dream your work helps to make real. About how so many of us work to buy our own freedom. This chapter is where the real power lies because I'll tell you a secret—none of us were born free.

At birth, we all require support to meet our most basic needs. As we get older and better acquainted with the world around us, our thirst for freedom grows. As adolescents, many of us scream and fight for our freedom, bucking against the authorities and systems that helped raise and groom us. You know the proverbial battle cry: "You can't tell me what to do!" In most cases, the system eventually wins as we surrender to a life bound by the walls of our societal positions and propped up by educational footholds.

Your freedom is something you have to consciously, deliberately, and consistently stake your claim to and defend. Adult freedom builds ladders and climbs over walls. It starts from the inside and works its way out. You start by mastering yourself because if you don't, somebody else will.

In the previous chapter, you developed a vision of who you want to be, but before we can start becoming, we need to take a more in-depth look at what a *who* is and what it means to *be*.

Who are you? Ultimately, you are what you do, say, and think. That's what it means to be a human being—a *who* who *is*—so it follows that changing those component parts changes the whole. Change what you do, say, and think, and you change who you are. In the reserved construction: to change who you are, change what you think, say, and do.

BEING LEADS TO DOING AND HAVING

As a young man leaving school, I thought about my future and had no trouble knowing what I wanted to have and do. I could rattle off a list of possessions and experiences I wanted to have. I could even imagine myself having them—driving my Porsche 911 along a scenic riverfront before taking my private plane for a weekend escape in Napa Valley and coming back home to an executive job I didn't hate. I could see it; it just didn't feel like me. That guy wasn't who I was. My imaginings didn't fit my identity.

Trying to forge a reality that's incongruent with who you are isn't sustainable. You may make some progress but it inevitably stalls out and you end up back where you started—or worse. Likewise, most of the people who win the lottery don't stay rich for long. They aren't rich people; they're just poor folks with a lot of money for a little while. Having and doing come from being. If you aren't rich in your mind and habits, you'll behave yourself right back to where you were, no matter how much money lands in your lap.

Don't be committed to the outcome; be committed to the process. Do what it takes.

On some level, most of us know that if we do what it takes, we'll get what we want. But to do what it takes, you have to *be* the kind of person who does what it takes. We think being rich comes from having money, which comes from doing whatever it takes, but being is the *be*ginning, not the outcome. If who you are is committed, focused, dedicated, and deserving, you'll take the actions that will deliver the outcomes. The trick is bringing who you are into alignment with what you want, and that starts with understanding what (and how) you think.

HAND-ME-DOWN SELVES

With all the best of intentions, our parents spoon-fed us the American dream, and we gobbled it up. We also metabolized their thoughts. (Maybe this is why parenting is so tiring: our kids are eating our minds.) If you were told to be a big boy and not cry, when you feel tears threatening as an adult, you're very likely to tell yourself some version of "Man up!" The thought feels like yours, but it isn't. You were trained to think just like you were trained to use the toilet. Your thoughts aren't innate.

Obviously, we don't want to strip ourselves down to our original thinking or bathroom habits. It's only necessary to recognize how much of what you think, say, and do comes from hand-me-down scripts and how little is actually hardwired. Your parents taught you to go to the bathroom, but what you do once you're there is biologically given. The biological needs of your body, your impulses, and emotions are instincts on full-time autopilot. Short of undergoing substantial reconditioning, those behaviors are out of your control. Pretty much everything else you think, say, or do is up for grabs. But how much is there? In the next section, we'll take an inventory.

The educational pipeline teaches us to answer the questions it asks. We move faster and rise higher depending on how many of our answers are correct. This emphasizes generating answers, not asking questions; correctness, not creativity; and results, not processes. Many of us carry this correct-answer meta-education into planning our lives, believing that we'll win if we can just do everything right. But life isn't a contest, and the only finish line is the grave. It's okay not to have answers, and correct is relative and personal. What's the correct answer to "What's for dinner tonight?" Is it reasonable to think it would be the same every day or for everyone in the world (or even everyone in your family)?

As you inventory your thoughts, words, and actions, try to operate without the hand-me-down meta-thought that there are right answers to the questions I put to you. Treat them as an investigation, not an inquisition.

YOUR TURN: INVENTORY

Pause for a moment and think about your thinking. Are you thinking about the future vision of yourself you created in the last chapter? Are you thinking about your past? Are you thinking about getting a sandwich? Once you've identified what you're thinking about, assess *how* you're thinking. Are your thoughts optimistic or gloomy, practical or abstract? When it's not occupied with something pressing, what does your mind drift to? Are you writing shopping lists or stage plays in your head? Are you thinking about your kids when you're in budget meetings, or do you think about work when you're playing checkers with your kids? Beginning to pay attention to the content and quality of your thoughts is the first part of the first step of becoming.

The second part is to become aware of what you say and how you say it. Do you talk about what's possible, or do you complain about the way things are? Do you talk about big ideas or the weather? Are you more likely to praise or criticize, ask questions or monologue? How do you think people feel after talking with you? Do they leave encouraged or demoralized, revved up or dragged down? What are the five words in heaviest rotation in your vocabulary? Try to imagine counting up all the words you say in a week. Once you get rid of the articles, prepositions, and conjunctions, what words do you use most frequently? Most of us have a small set of go-to words (or expletives) we primarily use to express emotion. We also have topics we gravitate toward. What are yours?

Finally, inventory your regular actions. What habits do you have? What routine behaviors do you perform? What are five things you do every day? What do you do most frequently in a single day? Are there things you only do on the weekends, but then give them twenty hours in two days? What do you just not feel okay if you don't do? What do you catch yourself doing without having consciously decided to do? When you find yourself with a free hour, what are you most likely to do? What do you do when you're supposed to be doing something else?

Once you're clear on *what* you're doing, ask *how*. How do you do what you do? Do you go all in, fully present and totally focused, or do you do things grudgingly, with partial focus, or to the minimum acceptable standard? Do you get every detail right, or do you work in broad strokes? Take a moment to make a list of what you're doing and how you're doing those tasks.

You should now have a pretty comprehensive grasp of your habits of thought, speech, and action. These are the things you're most likely to continue to think, say, and do in the days, weeks, and years to come.

How does that feel? Do you feel good about the idea that these habits will still be with you in five years? Do they fit into that vision you've created for your future? Will they get you there? Will the path you walk today get you where you want to be tomorrow? Let's find out.

WHAT WOULD ASPIRATIONAL YOU DO?

Are any of your thoughts, words, or actions moving you further away from where you want to go and who you want to be? If so, take a good, hard look at them. What you think, say, and do not only determine who you are, but they also prove what you value. If things that are a part of your current life don't fit into the picture of your ideal future self, either you've discovered something important that needs to be added to your aspirational self or you have a bad habit.

Eliminate the Negative

You can't move forward until you cut the dead weight. Get rid of your bad habits and dump the emotional baggage you've been carrying around. I'm not saying this will be easy, simple, or fast, but it *will* be extremely worthwhile.

Make a plan to stop thinking, saying, and doing things that take you further from your aspirational self. Start with your list of habits and identify the behaviors that would be most impactful to eliminate. What behavior would have the greatest immediate impact on who you're trying to become and where you're trying to go? We don't want to tackle all of the bad habits at one time. It's hard enough to acknowledge them. Use this approach to prioritize your effort. Then let's get to work!

If you're struggling with bad habits that your body reinforces in the form of addiction, you may need a community of other people who are doing the same important work. Check out your local branch of AA or google your location with the word "recovery." You aren't broken or bad, and it's not too late.

Even without the added weight of addiction, habits are a hard skin to shed. Accountability buddies can offer a deep well of support, as can professional therapists.

Beyond support from friends or skilled professionals, there are many tools and resources available to help you improve your habits. Results will vary from person to person, but you owe it to yourself to find what works for you. If you need detailed help to make substantive change, James Clear's best-selling book *Atomic Habits* does a phenomenal job of illuminating both the science and strategy of changing habits. I highly recommend it!

Implement the Positive

Every day, you make thousands of choices—when to wake up, what to eat, whether to exercise. If you move even a fraction of those choices closer to what your aspirational self would do, you'll take a significant step toward becoming who you want to be.

What would it sound like inside the head of your aspirational self? This person you've imagined, what do they think about? What is the content and quality of their thoughts? Think one of their thoughts right now.

What kind of things does your aspirational self talk about? What do they say every day? How do they speak to the significant people in their lives? Start saying some of that today.

What does your aspirational self do every morning that you could start doing tomorrow? How do you imagine your aspirational self starting their day? What part of their morning routine could you start doing tomorrow? As you continue to inventory your thoughts, words, and actions, evaluate them against what you think your aspirational self would think, say, and do. Then do that.

If you have trouble deciding what to do first, you can use the same impact-ease ranking system we used in the previous section.

Evaluate the Neutral

Once you've stopped doing, saying, and thinking things that pull you away from your aspirational self and have started thinking, saying, and doing things that move you closer to who you want most to be, look at what's left. Are there time-wasters (activities or people) who, while not negative, aren't adding anything to your life or growth? Leisure time is great, but are there things you can do for fun that might move you closer to who you want to be?

Rank these unnecessary, neutral aspects of your behavior according to which would be the easiest to stop doing and tackle that one first.

THE WRONG THING TO DO

While these elimination and implementation exercises can be very helpful, I also recommend that you don't get too bogged down in these lists. Here's the most important thing of all to know: doing nothing to move closer to your aspirational self is the only wrong thing to do.

SELF-MASTERY

Most people use the two words "response" and "reaction" interchangeably. That's perfectly understandable. They both describe what we do in the presence of stimuli. The critical difference between these two things is choice. Responses are freely chosen; reactions are spontaneous or trained behaviors performed without deliberate consideration.

While I'll always advocate for choice, reactions have a critical role to play. Responses and reactions are, in and of themselves, value-neutral.

If you see a car hurtling toward your children and you snatch them out of its path, that reaction is morally superior to considering your options. Premeditated murder might be a response, but that doesn't make it okay. To be truly free, we need to be our own master and maintain the value-neutral quality of our most primal reactions while choosing our responses to align with our aspirational selves.

RESPONSES AND REACTIONS IN ACTION

Imagine you're sitting on the bus on your way to an important job interview. The bus isn't crowded, so when a woman gets on with her son, you don't pay much attention. There are plenty of seats available, and you go back to running over your talking points for the big meeting. The mother passes you, distracted and talking on her cell phone, and the kid trips and dumps his cherry slushy on your shirt. You leap to your feet with a shout—an involuntary reaction. The slushy is freezing, your shirt is ruined, and anger floods through you.

What happens next is going to depend on several factors. If you haven't built a habit of stopping in the moment you feel your anger bubbling up, you aren't going to be able to respond, but choice has entered the equation. Because you don't have a habit of reacting to anger with a full stop to back yourself out and consider what your aspirational self would do in these circumstances, the choice is made by whatever habit you do have in place.

Your habitual reactions may feel involuntary, but they're not. What you think, say, and do when you're angry (or sad or hungry or excited) isn't any indication of who you are or a reflection of your character. It's often a result of your early training. Your reactions may be exactly like your dad's or the mirror opposite. They may be based on beliefs you internalized from your parents or peers, but you can take ownership here too. Whether you end up regretting things you do or say when you're angry, or if your reaction to stress is to drink heavily (and you'd prefer it weren't), the process of retraining your reactions is the same. Train yourself to detach from the situation, mentally if you can, physically if you need to. Only when your habitual reaction is to not react, can you begin to exercise your freedom to respond.

Let your vision of your aspirational self help you decide how to respond. Asking what your ideal future self would do in similar circumstances is a great way to make better choices, but not the only one. Think about the kind of person you want to be. If you value kindness and want to be kind, you can ask yourself what the kind response is. You can also consider outcomes. Which response is the most likely to move you closer to where you want to go?

Let's get back on our imaginary bus. What if, in the moment of your slushy baptism, your habitual reaction is to not react? You take a moment, a deep breath. If you realize you're just too angry to respond well, get off the bus. When our emotions are really stirred up, we temporarily lose access to the parts of our minds that make decisions and choose responses.

Whether you need just a few breaths or to walk a few blocks before you can think clearly again, once you're able to consider your response, let's imagine you go through our process. What would your aspirational self do? If you know, you can choose to do that. If you don't, think about who you want to be. If you value altruism, maybe you'll comfort the kid and reassure the mom. If you value innovation, you'll turn your creative mind to the problem at hand and devise a clever way to clean, replace, or hide your shirt.

If who you aspire to be doesn't offer any possible responses, ask yourself what would move you closer to what you want. If the job you're interviewing for is part of your plan to get where you want to go, choose the response that will help you the most in your interview. Could your stained and cherry-scented shirt make you memorable? Could you turn it into an ice-breaking (icy? Icee?) story?

RESPONSES AND REACTIONS IN PRACTICE

Pick one reaction you regularly have that isn't aligned with your aspirational self. Such gaps are the result of unsurfaced habitual thoughts, words, and actions that get triggered by any variety of circumstances and which, once triggered, run on autopilot. These reactions don't have to remain permanent. With intentional, consistent practice, we can evolve our instinctive reactions into refined responses.

As a jazz musician, there's nothing more exhilarating than playing a riveting solo in front of an audience. On the flip side, nothing is more disheartening than hearing a fan say, "We've heard that before. Play something new!" This usually happens when the musician has slacked off on practicing and is just playing based on instincts and old habits. A fellow musician told me once, "If I don't practice for one day, I can tell. If I don't practice for a week, my peers can tell. If I don't practice for a month, the audience can tell." This principle holds true for musicians and anyone who's on the journey to be BETTER.

Think carefully about your chain of triggers for this unwanted reaction. Which ones can you disarm? If your misaligned behavior is triggered by a thought you can identify, develop the more affirming words you want to replace it.

Now we're going to write a response plan to close the gap that exemplifies how your aspirational self would respond. Write this plan as an if-then statement. "If I'm thinking (thought), then I'll say (words)."

Here's what this might look like in action. If the way you eat isn't always aligned with your image of who you want to be, you might look at what you're thinking before eating foods that aren't good for you. It might be some variation of "so screw it." Maybe it goes something like this: "I've already blown my diet for today, so screw it; I might as well finish the ice cream." Or perhaps it's: "I've denied myself my favorite treats all week, and I still haven't lost the weight I wanted to, so screw it; I guess I'm just not meant to be skinny."

Your plan for replacing your reactions with a response might then be something like: If I find myself thinking, "So screw it," I'll say out loud, "My health and my weight are important to me, and I'm in charge of what I eat."

If you can't identify the thoughts that trigger a reaction you want to change, are there words you hear yourself say or that others say to you that set the reaction off? Create a response plan that follows up those words with a different, chosen behavior. You can use "When I say (words), I'll (action)" if it resonates more than an if-then statement.

For example, let's say you find yourself shouting at your kids in a way your kind and patient aspirational self wouldn't. Any thoughts you have before the yelling starts seem to come straight out of your mouth without being thought first, but you notice that you always habitually say something before the tirade really gets going. Maybe it's, "Now, listen up!" Or, "I've had about enough!" Or, "For the last time!"

Your response plan might be: When I hear myself saying, "I've had about enough!" I'll go pour myself a glass of water and drink the entire thing. (It's hard to yell with your mouth full.)

If your self-awareness only returns once you're already in action, you need to look for environmental triggers and make a response plan that includes avoiding or preemptively ending your exposure. Match the intensity of your response to the danger of the action.

For example, if the first glass of wine regularly makes the second glass sound like a good idea, and you often find yourself having two or three glasses on nights you really only intended to have one, you might start pouring tonight's glass in the morning. At a time when wine is easy to resist, pour an amount that's congruent with your aspirational self into an empty bottle and put the rest in the garage or even the trunk of your car if you have to. Preplanning makes it possible to behave virtuously without actually being virtuous.

THE PATH OF MY BECOMING

Getting clarity around who you want to be improves your discernment. It's easier to do the right things, avoid the wrong things, and tell the difference between them. Knowing that I cared about money and wanted to take care of my family but didn't put much value on reaching the next predetermined financial milestone, I had much less trouble leaving for the day when my work was finished. Because I was moving closer to where I wanted to be, I was increasingly in places or situations I'd chosen, rather than feeling like I was only doing things because I had to. This isn't to say every day was a Sunday in a park full of sunshine and kites, but I wasn't crying on the freeway anymore, either.

This began by identifying the threads that ran through my life and weaving them into a purpose that shaped who I was. I knew I was an innovator, that I enjoyed being creative, and that I believed in economic and social freedom.

Developing my aspirational self, I incorporated those values, passions, gifts, and skills. I envisioned a future self who builds companies, plays music, and empowers people. I began to see that, although my job was great, it wasn't great for me. I fit in there just fine, but it wasn't where I belonged. I chose my deliberate response as an exercise in self-mastery and becoming.

I started talking about music again. Sometimes, when I was working on a song at home, I'd share it with someone at the office. When I had a show, I invited my coworkers and clients. I began making references to music and using it both for analogies and for mood shifting. When I led meetings, I'd have just the right song playing as people arrived and got settled.

The tone of a meeting changes when it starts out with a Miles Davis tune. People get a little more upbeat with an up-tempo soundtrack. They file in with a bit more swagger and smile more. They're just a little bit cooler than they were before they walked through the door. Music became a bridge between professional contacts and personal relationships. A client who comes to a gig is going to answer your calls. If I spend two minutes in the office with someone sharing a song, we're already in sync, matching the same rhythm.

I started getting more agreement at work and had more successes. I deployed the improvisational skills I'd honed with music at work. I'm not going to say my colleagues and I started making beautiful music together because I'd have to put a dollar in the bad joke jar, but you get the picture. My team and I worked more harmoniously. The people I worked *for*, not so much.

I didn't care. I knew I was still performing as well—better—than I had from behind my corporate mask, and my boss wasn't my master. Masters can prohibit music; as my own master, I embraced and amplified it.

Today, I'm living my purpose in my business life and my music—helping people live lives worth remembering. I coach entrepreneurs in making the decisions and building the companies that create value and positive change in the world and help position them to be their best selves and take their next best step. I got where I am (and am still heading where I want to go) by letting the gap between who I was and who I wanted to be power my becoming.

WHO ARE YOU BECOMING?

Continue to pay attention to the content and quality of your thoughts, to what you say and how you say it, and to your habits. Watch out for opportunities to eliminate the things that move you further from your aspirational self and implement ones that hasten your becoming.

Use that response plan. It will help you become **BETTER** by claiming your freedom to make choices, by choosing responses that move you closer to your aspirational self, and by mastering your present self—your thoughts, words, and actions.

Looking at myself in the bathroom mirror, I knew I had to start doing things differently. The decision to do so was the beginning of my becoming. It was also the start of discovering the three steps we've just worked together. But if you've been paying attention, you know we're not done. Becoming is a lifelong process. It isn't about fixing you (you're not broken), and it's not about having whatever you've chosen to be and do in the direction of attaining. The point is the process of ongoing becoming.

You're not going to wake up tomorrow as your aspirational self, and even if you did, the very nature of that self would have already fashioned an aspirational self of its own. We truly never arrive. We keep taking the next step forever on the best path toward who we are becoming.

Chapter 7

STEP 4(EVER): THE PATH FORWARD

A shocking 70 percent of lottery winners go bankrupt *after* they win the lottery. They certainly have the resources to hire competent money managers, but they usually don't because they don't know better (or have the maturity to budget wisely). A similar phenomenon can happen when people reach their weight loss and fitness aspirations. Getting fit is hard, but people still succeed at it. Sadly, however, few of them maintain what they worked so hard to accomplish. Getting what you want isn't all you want. You want to be able to *keep* it.

It won't always be easy. A life of ongoing becoming is like living between two TV shows with similar names but decades apart—*American Gladiators* and *American Ninja Warrior.* Don't laugh.

Okay, you can laugh. I'm a fitness nut and I loved both shows. But for this analogy and the images I'll invoke (especially of *Gladiators* with their 1980s hair and headbands, giant weaponized Q-tips, and Lycra mankinis) you're in for a good chuckle at the least. But they'll also stick with you, and when you land on your back in life's foam pit, I hope you'll remember both the smile and the simile.

Life is like these two TV shows. Sometimes, you're on *American Ninja Warrior,* facing a daunting obstacle. You race against the clock, calling on your reserves of personal fortitude to overcome your challenges, with the cheers of the crowd helping push you forward. Other days, you're back in the '80s, in a leotard that has a more intimate relationship with your sphincter than most of us would be comfortable with today.

On gladiator days, you're not facing inert obstacles nor is the crowd cheering you on—people are out to get you! You're competing against other players for the fastest time, the highest score, and the greatest glory. But your peers and the laws of physics aren't your only problem. You're also contending with professional gladiators—menacing mammoths and intimidating amazons—whose only job is to look great in tights and to ruin your day. These full-time athletes aren't trying to get there first or protect their title. All they want to do is knock you down and keep you from getting where you're trying to go. Life feels like that some days. And when it does, remember: you only have one job, too. Keep putting one foot in front of the other, knowing that each step brings you that much closer to who you are becoming. When you get knocked down, you get back up. You have a clear vision of who you want to be and how to keep becoming it, and you have better hair. Unless you're like me... and I hope God blessed you with a well-shaped head.

Having accepted who you are, with a clear vision of both who you want to be and what the path between here and there looks like, you have to start (and continue) moving forward. Seven principles form the guardrails that can keep you on track (and out of foam pits).

In our final chapter together, I'll introduce you to the seven states of **BEING** to become **BETTER**, sequenced to get you started and keep you going.

BE INTENTIONAL

There is no success without intent.

Without a goal or desired outcome, anything good that happens is just a happy accident. While we certainly prefer happy accidents to the other kind, luck isn't the same as success. Luck just happens. Success is intentional.

Growing up, my mom told me there are three types of people: those that watch things happen, those that make things happen, and those that wonder what happened. Only one of these persons is successful. The others are observantly lucky or obliviously unfortunate.

Once you have a clear vision of your aspirational self and have made a clear and conscious decision to deliberately do the things that move you closer to your vision and to stop doing the things that take you further from it, you satisfy this first principle. Congratulations. That's huge. Life is no longer just happening to you.

Being intentional can manifest as a written list of yearly goals or daily to-do (or don't-do) lists. It can be an internal and regularly renewed commitment to responding more than reacting and choosing your responses based on moving closer to your aspirational self.

BE COMMITTED

The journey is long, and change doesn't happen overnight. In fact, the process is more important than the end product. Commitment is essential to becoming because if you haven't committed fully, you won't be able to persevere in the face of obstacles, setbacks, disappointments, and the occasional gladiator.

Commitment is one of the hardest attributes to embody because it can't be taught or bought. You can't force someone to commit to anything, just as you can't buy your own willingness to stick it out. It's why maturity is the final filter on our "best" behaviors. Commitment is the fruit of your maturity. It asks that you fall in love with the process more than the outcome and that you push beyond lost battles in order to win the war.

As a young man, I was taught a poem by John Greenleaf Whittier that fully embodies commitment. I share it with you as a reminder of what commitment looks like and to encourage you.

Don't Quit

When things go wrong as they sometimes will,
When the road you're trudging seems all up hill,
When the funds are low and the debts are high
And you want to smile, but you have to sigh,
When care is pressing you down a bit,
Rest if you must, but don't you quit.
Life is strange with its twists and turns
As every one of us sometimes learns
And many a failure comes about
When he might have won had he stuck it out;
Don't give up though the pace seems slow—
You may succeed with another blow.
Success is failure turned inside out—
The silver tint of the clouds of doubt,
And you never can tell just how close you are,
It may be near when it seems so far;
So stick to the fight when you're hardest hit—
It's when things seem worst that you must not quit.

—JOHN GREENLEAF WHITTIER

BE HEALTHY

To make better choices, you need to build your capacity by feeding your BETTER nature. Feed your mind, body, and spirit. Everything you consume affects you, so you have to adjust your inputs to be conducive to your desired outcomes and increase your capacity to move toward them.

I often advise entrepreneurs and business leaders on what it takes to build a healthy business. There's no silver bullet! It's truly a modern miracle. It's the intersection of a great idea with the right team, the right market at the right time, reasonably priced resources that can be developed, packaged, and sold for a profit. Take away any one of those variables, and at best you have a provocative enterprise struggling to survive.

Imagine if Facebook launched in 1980. The evolution of technology wasn't there to support the business. But place Mark Zuckerberg on the campus of Harvard University in 2002 with the right team, and twenty years later we have one of the most influential companies in modern history.

As you grow daily, you need a balanced diet of inputs and environments to become closer to your aspirational self.

Food

I'm sure you've heard the expression "you are what you eat," and while it may seem at odds with my claim that we are what we think, say, and do, it really isn't. Everything—and I mean everything—you do, including thinking, burns calories. (Thinking, in fact, requires quite a lot of energy, which is why we evolved to do so little of it, outsourcing as many decisions as possible to our habits or reactions.) You need calories to think, say, and do the things that define you. The better quality your calories are, the better your thoughts, words, and actions will be; and the better they are, the BETTER you are.

Now, I'm not telling you to give up Snickers. Snickers are delicious, but a Snickers a day isn't likely on your nutritionist's recommended diet.

Obviously, I'm not a doctor or a nutritionist, and if you need more detailed or customized advice on what constitutes better eating for you, please see a professional! But in general, better food means a good balance and a wide variety of high-quality ingredients, minimally processed and low in refined sugar and trans fats.

Content

Media can affect our moods. If your aspirational self is a peaceful, calm person, but your devices deliver a constant stream of speed metal or street fight videos, you're probably going to have more anger to master before you can respond rather than react to events in your environment.

Books, TV, and movies can introduce us to new perspectives and emotions, positive and negative, or to nothing at all. The internet can introduce us to almost anything. Be intentional about what you consume.

People

Don't eat people. No, really—don't eat people! We all tend to absorb the attitudes, jargon, and habits of the people we're around most. In fact, the best indication of whether you'll be overweight is the BMI of the five people with whom you spend the most time. Hanging out with high-energy, positive people who talk about interesting things and engage in healthy activities is much more likely to move you toward your aspirational future self than listening to people complain about mundane things while drinking beer.

Look at the people you spend the most time with. Where are they headed? Do you want to go there? Are they more like you'd like to be or less?

Environments

We're also affected by the places where we spend our time. Bleak, low-light, cold places aren't likely to put you in a cheerful, bright, warm mood. It's hard to be creative in sterile environments and easy to be distracted in chaotic ones. Unsurprisingly, people who spend time at the gym tend to be more fit than people who don't.

Think about the places where you do your work and live your life. Are they conducive to the person you want to be? Can you imagine your aspirational self living and working in them? Are your spaces set up to enable or encourage you to do the things you want to do? If your guitar is on a stand by the TV, you're more likely to play it when you crash on the sofa than if it's in the closet upstairs.

BE ACCOUNTABLE

If self-mastery is all about owning the thoughts, words, and actions that define you, accountability is about owning the results. You will stumble on the path of your becoming. Sometimes, you'll fall into old reactions rather than choosing your responses. Other times, you'll succeed in responding, but your thoughts, words, or actions will fail to produce the outcome you thought they would. That's fine. It's inevitable. (More on this in a minute.)

Remember way back in Chapter 3, when I said where you are in the best place you can be? It's still true. You can only do as well as you know how to do with the resources you have available and the maturity you can muster. You did the best you could possibly do. If you've come this far, it's because you took on that responsibility and started working to be something better. (Take a moment to be proud of that!)

You took responsibility for doing better, and look at the progress you've made! Owning your outcomes and claiming responsibility is an incredibly powerful thing to do. It increases the territory of your freedom. When you're accountable, you're in control. As soon as you blame anyone or anything, you're shifting responsibility to them, and with it some portion of your freedom. To give up responsibility is to give up control. To say your boss made you angry is to say he mastered your emotions. Don't give away that kind of power.

BE PRESENT

Being fully present means showing up with your whole self every day. You don't hedge your bets or leave the back door open; you go all in. You don't take your body one place while your mind goes somewhere else; you bring your full attention to each moment. You don't arrive late, leave early, or skip days; you're slow, steady, and consistent.

Your presence is a gift to yourself, your people, and the situations that you encounter. It's impossible to do your best work while you're divided.

Not only will you not achieve the desired results, but you'll also put yourself and others at risk. Imagine trying to bench press with just one hand on the barbell while you scroll social media with the other hand. You may be able to lift the bar off the rack, but the likelihood of you dropping the weight on your neck is substantially higher. The picture might go viral, but you won't be there to enjoy it.

Being present sets you up for success and for more memorable moments. Now doesn't that sound better?

BE BETTER (NOT PERFECT)

Perfect sounds desirable, and certainly striving for perfection is part of the American dream, but perfection is a dead end (or death itself). Perfection means there's nowhere else to go, nothing left to want—you've peaked, and it's all downhill from there.

Drop the goal of perfection and set your aim on a lifetime of growth. Remember, the journey only stops at the grave—you don't want to arrive early! You want to be continually finding new paths of improvement, new avenues of growth.

Occasionally, you will reach a summit, a place where it seems impossible for things to get better. Stop and enjoy the view. Throw your arms in the air and shout at the sky. You've made it! You've accomplished a goal or mastered some aspect of your life. Enjoy every moment of triumph.

From the top of the mountain, there aren't a lot of possible trajectories. If there's nothing above you (which is kind of the definition of "peak"), it can look like the only options are to cling to the summit or tumble down. The fall is terrifying, and the higher up you've climbed, the more you'll believe the drop would be fatal. It won't be. You've survived other plunges. But the fear of it can be petrifying. You stop exploring, stop taking risks, stop reaching out, and lie face down, holding on to the earth for dear life. And missing out on the wonderful view.

But there's another option. If you can't go up and have less than no interest in coming down, you can leap from your current peak to a new mountain. You may not start at a parallel position when you zip-line or glide to the next challenge, but you've proved yourself more than capable. It takes a lot of courage to leave a pinnacle of success to throw yourself onto another mountain. Luckily, you've had plenty of practice being brave by now. Find a new challenge to conquer, a new path to a different better.

BE HEROIC

But what if you never seem to reach that distant peak? You're committed. You get back up when you're knocked down. If you play video games, you know what to do next—plunder the bodies of your enemies for treasure.

If you'd like a gentler image, think about your favorite rom-com or fairy tale. After the race to the airport or the quest object is found, what happens? The hero returns to their group of friends or their village changed in a way that benefits their community. They become a husband or wife, king or queen, and their friends or subjects prosper.

We gain something valuable from struggling. I'm a comic book fan, so for me, the most resonant stories are about superheroes.

In every superhero's origin story (and remember, there's always an origin story), the superhero gets bitten, mutated, or scarred by tragedy before beginning a life-altering journey toward self-discovery. As we discussed in Chapter 2, the injury is the source of the gift, but the journey is where the magic happens.

During that journey, the hero meets a challenge that seems insurmountable—the villain that's too strong or the mountain too tall to scale. But it's in their darkest hour when the hero makes that one, seemingly small decision to not quit—to continue the fight despite overwhelming odds—that they discover their true superpowers. It's only in pushing *past* the urge to throw in the towel that they find they possess superhuman strength or the gift of flight. Pain is both the obstacle and the key that unlocks the greatness within.

Think of the pain you were in when you started reading. Whatever caused it, that pain motivated you to make some changes—pain is fuel for growth—and the lesson I want you to take from that is this: struggle is how we get to the good stuff. Go ahead and embrace it.

Embrace the struggle, and discover your superpowers.

Personal growth is just like muscle growth. You have to do hard things more times than you think you can. You have to resist one last temptation, do one more bicep curl, and push through the resistance. We build strength by forcing small tears in our muscle fiber so our bodies can stitch them together, bigger for the added thread. We are stronger in the places we have healed.

FROM BEHIND THE MASK

The difference between the paint on the wall and the paint on an artist's canvas is the homogeneity in the first and its absence in the second. Antiquated organizations often ask us to hide our differences behind a mask and slice off the bits of our personalities and enthusiasms that threaten to overflow our cubicles. Still, even in the stodgiest of companies, uniformity isn't what gets celebrated. Although any variation or innovation may be suspect or even attacked until it succeeds, it's heralded and called out once it does. We are attracted to difference, even when it scares us. The truth is, we need difference… even in the corporate world.

In a green field, it's the solitary orange poppy your eye will pick out from the million blades of grass. It's what's different in each of us that makes us beautiful. It's what doesn't fit about you that makes you remarkable. Human beings aren't cast from a mold to be interchangeable as batteries or envelopes (and even they come in different sizes).

When you take off your mask, you begin to contribute what only you can to the world. You add your individual voice to that human choir that's so much richer for its multiplicity than one voice—even Lady Day's—multiplied a million times.

There's a unique space where each of us fits, a role that we're each meant to play. When we do the work we were put here to do in the space where our unique passions and gifts, skills, and interests lead us, we can't help but contribute something no one else can. Because your true face is unique, because you are different from every other being that has ever been or ever will be, you must be exactly and completely yourself. When you invest in continually becoming a better you, you improve the world for all of us. An inspired life inspires others. Your being **BETTER** begins our becoming, and together we cocreate a better being for us all.

FOREVER BECOMING

Becoming begins with intention. You create a vision of your aspirational self, and you deliberately determine and intentionally choose to do those things that move you closer to who and where you want to be. Then you commit to doing them every day, whether you want to or not when you're tired or frustrated. You commit to sticking it out, getting back up when you're down, and never, ever stopping. You consume the food and content that supports your commitment and spend time with the people and in the environments that align with your intentions. You're accountable for your progress and take responsibility for your missteps. You bring your whole self to everything you do and constantly strive for better, not perfection. And you welcome the struggle knowing that that's how heroes become heroes. Or gladiators.

When I stopped working to buy my freedom and instead chose to be free, I quit hoping to be moved from the field to the house. I stopped being the company man and declared myself a free one. I dropped my corporate mask and fully embraced the man in the mirror. Proudly, I am freely me every day, and I want to empower freedom everywhere. The world is a better place when we let our authentic selves shine brightly. If you won't reveal your genius and activate your superpowers for yourself, do it for your family. Do it for your friends. Do it for me.

The world doesn't need more unquestionably obedient cogs. It needs the color and flavor that only you can bring. You're the difference between what's always been and what's always been possible. We all need who you're **BECOMING**.

CONCLUSION

When I'm on stage, I'm serving three masters—the music, the audience, and my highest self. To me, music—Music—comes from the better world of ideals, the home of powerful forces like Freedom and Faith. It's something powerful and abstract. It is spiritual and transcendent, and part of my work is to be as worthy and as skillful a conduit as I can be for its coming into the room. I'm carrying it to the people, and it's carrying me. Together, we're creating one of two things for the folks who've come to see it. When I play, I'm the experience or the soundtrack. Either way, I'm living my purpose. If a person is there to see the show, giving the music their full attention, I'm going to deliver a performance worth remembering. If they're there on their first date or twentieth anniversary, their eyes on each other, I'm not going to pull focus; I'm there to score the moment and add to its depth. I've tried to deliver the same thing for you here.

Maybe my words have been a soundtrack, coloring your life experiences as you read. Maybe you came to the (book) club to catch every note.

As long as we're occupying the same space, breathing God's good air together, your freedom is part of my purpose. I've shared my story from my grandparents to my kitchen floor and back to give you an intimate look into my own becoming. We've delved into the history of the American dream and the education pipeline to see who's buying and selling and to get a better understanding of how arbitrary and disingenuous their promises are. And you began to question what your dream of the good life might be.

We took a look at origin stories and saw the way heroes are forged from the tragedies and accidents that befall them. We talked about why they (and we) wear masks and what those false faces of convenience can do to our unique and individual beauty. I invited you to examine what your corporate mask hides, who benefits, and how much it hurts you to cram yourself behind its restrictive façade or into its tiny shoes.

We discussed what happens when the mask fractures and looked at the crippling power of shame to keep us isolated, hiding our cracking-apart selves from the world and our own awareness. I told you why it isn't your fault. We began building an understanding of how the things you know, the resources you have, and the maturity you've achieved limit or expand what's possible. We started talking about what BETTER could mean and why you can (and should) accept even what you cannot stand about yourself and your life.

As we started working the steps together, your workload increased. You made an inventory of your past and your people. You wrote a personal history, looking for patterns and themes and unburdening yourself of your past's unhelpful baggage. As you moved forward, you constructed an aspirational self, vision-casting an ideal unique to you and purpose-built to include what you want to have, do, and be. You identified your passions, gifts, and skills, your people, and your causes. You started looking at those fruitful places where they intersect. Then we leveraged the power of your aspirational self to start becoming.

As you increased your self-mastery and moved from reacting from habit or programming to choosing your responses, you learned to test steadily more of your decisions against the standard of your aspiration. You got rid of negative habits and implemented positive ones. You learned to monitor what you think, say, and do, expanding your freedom by making more and better choices.

If you've answered the questions and done the exercises, we've begun a collaboration that I hope lasts a long time. Reach out to me. Share your story on *BETTER*'s companion website, www.JeffPonders.com/better.

Once you've reassembled the fractured parts of yourself and started taking your whole self everywhere, options open up, possibilities expand, and there's no limit to who you can be, what you can do, and how many people you can positively impact. Our lives are our testimony. Once you've claimed your freedom, your BETTER life is a promise and a challenge to others to do the same.

Drop the mask and uncover your brilliance.

Escape the corporate nightmare and own your freedom.

Stop dreaming about tomorrow, and make "one day" today.

Add your voice to the choir and your becoming to a **BETTER** world. It needs you.

Lightning Source UK Ltd.
Milton Keynes UK
UKHW010052011022
409740UK00008B/184/J